Quick Reference Guide

Dictation Disc Company

14 East 38 Street, New York, NY 10016

Published by Dictation Disc Company

First Dictation Disc Printing

ISBN: 1-56243-031-9

10 9 8 7 6 5 4

Printed in the United States of America

INTRODUCTION

Quick Reference Guide for LOTUS 1-2-3 version 3.1+ will save you hours searching through technical manuals for keystrokes. Each function is illustrated with step-by-step key graphics to walk you through procedures. The template featured on the back cover will provide a fast reference to LOTUS 1-2-3 function keys.

A complete unit on WYSIWYG, the "What You See Is What You Get" feature, is included on pages 161-199.

An index, referencing all procedures covered in the book, appears on pages 236-245. A command index can be found on pages 231-235, while a description of functions appears on pages 200-213.

A glossary of spreadsheet terminology appears on pages 226-230.

Before you Begin

You should be familiar with the worksheet screen (illustrated on the following page), basic cursor movements and highlighting procedures. (Refer to pages 95-96, "Moving the Cell Cursor," and to page 79, "Highlighting Ranges" before proceeding.

Mouse actions for the WYSIWYG section will *not* be included in this reference guide.

It is our hope that this booklet will help you use LOTUS 1-2-3 with ease.

Iris Blanc
Zachary O. Auslander

Technical Editing:
Glenn S. Davis

Illustration of a Lotus 1-2-3 Spreadsheet

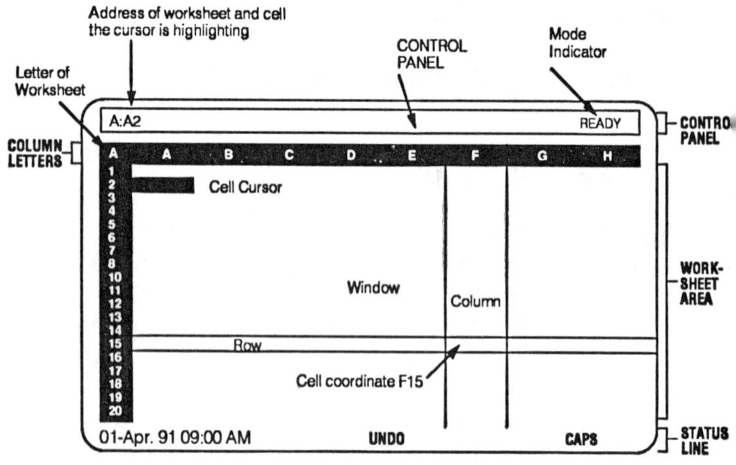

ADDING APPLICATION PROGRAMS

NOTE: • *Lotus 1-2-3 includes add-ins programs: Auditor, Backsolver, Viewer, and Wysiwyg.*
• *Add-in programs contain the extension .PLC.*
• *Check to determine the memory necessary to run add-in programs.*

Loading an Add-In Program

1. Press **Alt + F10** (Addin) .... Alt + F10
2. Press **L** (Load) L
3. Highlight add-in program to be loaded.
4. **ENTER** .... ↵
5. Select a key option to invoke add-in program:

   N (No-Key) Does not assign any key to invoke .... N

   1 Assign add-in to Alt+F7 key ... 1

   2 Assign add-in to Alt+F8 key ... 2

   3 Assign add-in to Alt+F9 key ... 3

6. Proceed to step 2 to invoke add-in program.

   -OR- OR

   Press **Q** (Quit) .... Q
   to cancel operation.

(continued)

ADDING APPLICATION PROGRAMS (continued)

To Invoke Add-In Program

1. Press **Alt + F10** (Addin) .... Alt + F10
2. Press **I** (Invoke) I
3. Highlight add-in program to be loaded.

   NOTE: Read the application into memory before using it.

4. **ENTER** .... ↵

To Specify Add-In Settings

NOTE: This feature will assign add-in files to be read automatically into memory, and applications to be started or assigned to keys automatically. This feature can also specify the default add-in directory.

1. Press **Alt + F10** (Addin) .... Alt + F10
2. Press **S** (Settings) .... S
3. Select a setting:

   S (System) to specify 1-2-3/Add-In startup procedure. .... S

   - Press **S** (Set) .... S
     to specify add-in file to be read into memory with 1-2-3.
   - Highlight add-in file.

(continued)

ADDING APPLICATION PROGRAMS (continued)

- **ENTER**.. ↵
- Press **Y** (Yes) .... Y
  to automatically start application
  when read into memory.

-OR- OR

- Type **N** (No).. N
  to not start application when
  read into memory.

- Select a key option to invoke the program:

  N (No-key)............................ N

  1 1

  2 2

  3 3

-OR- OR

- Press **C** (Cancel) C
- Highlight add-in file to be
  removed from setting.
- **ENTER**.. ↵

-OR- OR

- Press **D** (Directory)......................... D
  to specify default add-in directory.

(continued)

ADDING APPLICATION PROGRAMS (continued)

- Type directory .... **Option**
- **ENTER** .... [↵]

-OR- OR

- Press **U** (Update) .... [U]
  to save system settings in
  add-in configuration file.

F (File) to specify add-ins to be read into memory with the current file. .... [F]

- Press **S** (Set) .... [S]
  to specify add-in file to be read
  into memory with the current file.
- Highlight file to be read into memory.
- **ENTER** .... [↵]
- Press **Y** (Yes) .... [Y]
  to automatically start application
  when read into memory.

-OR- OR

- Press **N** (No) .... [N]
  to **not** start application
  when read into memory.

-OR- OR

- Press **C** (Cancel) .... [C]
  to remove add-in from
  setting sheet for the file.

(continued)

ADDING APPLICATION PROGRAMS (continued)

- Highlight file to be removed from setting sheet.
- **ENTER**.. ↵

To Remove Add-In Program

NOTE: Removes an add-in from memory for current work session. To detach add-in from system, press ***Alt+F10*** *Setting Cancel.*

1. Press **Alt + F10** (Addin)........................... Alt + F10
2. Press **R** (Remove).. R
3. Highlight add-in program to be removed.
4. **ENTER**.. ↵

To Clear Add-In Programs

NOTE: Removes ***all*** *add-ins from memory for current work session. To detach add-in from system, press* ***Alt+F10*** *Setting Cancel.*

1. Press **Alt + F10** (Addin)........................... Alt + F10
2. Press **C** (Clear)... C

(continued)

ADDING APPLICATION PROGRAMS (continued)

To Create a Table of Add-In Programs

1. Press **Alt + F10** (Addin) .... Alt + F10
2. Press **T** (Table) .... T
3. Select table contents:

   @ (@ functions) .... @

   M (Macros) .... M

   A (Applications) .... A
4. Highlight table range.
5. **ENTER** .... ↵

USING AUDITOR

*NOTE: This **add-in** feature allows the operator to identify and check formulas in the worksheet.*

Attaching AUDITOR Add-In/Selecting Auditor Options

1. Press **Alt + F10** (Addin) .... Alt + F10
2. Press **L** (Load) L
3. Highlight **AUDITOR.PLC.**
4. **ENTER** .... ↵
5. **ENTER** .... ↵
   to not assign add-in to a key.
6. Press **I** (Invoke) I
7. Highlight **AUDITOR.**
8. **ENTER** .... ↵

   *NOTE: Change reporting method to "List" by editing settings: press **F2, M, L, ENTER***

9. Select an Auditor option:

   P (Precedents) Identifies all cells that provide data for a specified formula cell. .... P

(continued)

USING AUDITOR (continued)

- Type cell containing formula for which there might be precedents (cells that contain data the formula uses in its calculations).
- **ENTER** .... ↵
- Highlight blank range (without data) to receive list of precedents.
- **ENTER** .... ↵

D (Dependents) Identifies all cells that refer to a specified cell. .... D

- Type cell containing formula for which there might be dependents (cells that contain formulas that depend on the data in the specified cell).
- **ENTER** .... ↵
- Highlight blank range (without data) to receive list of dependents.
- **ENTER** .... ↵

F (Formulas) Identifies all cells containing formulas in the worksheet. .. F

- Highlight blank range (without data) to receive list of formulas.
- **ENTER** .... ↵

(continued)

USING AUDITOR (continued)

R (Recalc-List) Identifies formulas in order of recalculation.......... [R]

- Highlight blank range (without data) to receive list of formulas.
- **ENTER** .... [↵]

C (Circs) Identifies all cells involved in circular references. .... [C]

- Highlight blank range (without data) to receive list of formulas.
- **ENTER** .... [↵]

Q (Quit) Quits Auditor........................ [Q]

USING BACKSOLVER

*NOTE: This **add-in** feature allows the operator to perform "backward" what-if problems to a achieve a result from a formula cell.*

Attaching Backsolver Add-In/Selecting Backsolver Options

NOTE: Turn UNDO on to return the adjustable cell to original value using Backsolver.

1. Press **Alt + F10** (Addin) .... Alt + F10
2. Press **L** (Load) L
3. Highlight **BSOLVER.PLC.**
4. **ENTER** .... ↵
5. **ENTER** .... ↵
   to not assign add-in to a key.
6. Press **I** (Invoke) I
7. Highlight **BSOLVER.**
8. **ENTER** .... ↵
9. Press a backsolver option:

   F (Formula-Cell) Identifies cell containing formula in the worksheet .... F

   - Highlight or type address of formula cell.
   - **ENTER** .... ↵

(continued)

USING BACKSOLVER (continued)

V (Value) Identifies cell containing value in the worksheet........... [V]

- Type the formula or number for formula cell.
- **ENTER**.. [↵]

A (Adjustable) Identifies cell containing data that will be changed in the worksheet.............. [A]

- Highlight or type address of adjustable cell.
- **ENTER**.. [↵]

S (Solver) Produces answer based on data from adjustable cell, formula cell, and value........... [S]

Q (Quit) Quits Backsolver.................... [Q]

Cancelling A Command

1. Press .... Esc
   to backup one menu level or command step at a time.

   -OR- OR

   Press **Ctrl + Break** .... Ctrl + Break
   to completely stop a procedure.

CHANGING COLUMN WIDTH

NOTE: The column width default is 9 characters.

For Range of Adjacent Columns

1. Press / (Menu) .... /
2. Press **W** (Worksheet) .... W
3. Press **C** (Column) C
4. Press **C** (Column-Range) C
5. Press **S** (Set-Width) .... S
6. Highlight range of columns to be modified.
7. **ENTER** .... ↵

8. Press right or left arrow key to desired column width. .... → or ←

   -OR- OR

   Type a number of desired column width .... **Option**
9. **ENTER** .... ↵

For Single Column

1. Press / (Menu) .... /
2. Press **W** (Worksheet) .... W

(continued)

CHANGING COLUMN WIDTH (continued)

3. Press **C** (Column) C
4. Press **S** (Set-Width) .... S
5. Press right or left arrow key to desired column width .... → or ←

   -OR- OR

   Type a number of desired column width .... **Option**
6. **ENTER** .... ↵

For Global Worksheet

1. Press **/** (Menu) .... /
2. Press **W** (Worksheet) .... W
3. Press **G** (Global) .... G
4. Press **C** (Column-Width) C
5. Press right or left arrow key to desired column width .... → or ←

   -OR- OR

   Type a number of desired column width .... **Option**
6. **ENTER** .... ↵

(continued)

CHANGING COLUMN WIDTH (continued)

Resetting Column Width

NOTE: Restores default column width to 9 characters.

For Adjacent Columns

1. Place cursor in first cell to be modified.
2. Press / (Menu) .... /
3. Press **W** (Worksheet) .... W
4. Press **C** (Column) C
5. Press **C** (Column-Range) C
6. Press **R** (Reset-Width) .... R
7. Highlight range of columns to be reset.
8. **ENTER** .... ↵

For Single Columns

1. Place cursor in first cell to be modified.
2. Press / (Menu) .... /
3. Press **W** (Worksheet) .... W
4. Press **C** (Column) C
5. Press **R** (Reset-Width) .... R

CHANGING A DIRECTORY

NOTE: This procedure will override the default directory for the current session only.

1. Press **/** (Menu) .... /
2. Press **F** (File) .... F
3. Press **D** (Directory) .... D
4. **ENTER** .... ↵
   to accept displayed directory.

   -OR- OR

   - Type a new directory.
   - **ENTER** .... ↵

COMBINING FILES

Copying Data

NOTE: Data is copied from the disk onto the current worksheet at the cursor location.

1. Place cursor on cell where data to be copied is to begin.
2. Press **/** (Menu) .... /
3. Press **F** (File) .... F
4. Press **C** (Combine) C
5. Press **C** (Copy) C
6.
   - Press **E** (Entire file) .... E
     to copy all data in a file on disk to current worksheet.
   - Highlight file to be copied.

   -OR- OR

   - Press **N** (Named/specified-range) .... N
     to copy data in a range in a file on disk to current worksheet.
   - Type range name.
   - **ENTER** .... ↵
   - Highlight file to be copied.
7. **ENTER** .... ↵

(continued)

COMBINING FILES (continued)

Adding Data

NOTE: • *Adds numbers and the results of numeric formulas in a saved worksheet file to numbers and blank cells in the current worksheet.*
• *File/Combine Add works with numeric data only.*
• *Numbers are changed from the disk onto the current worksheet at the cursor location.*

1. Place cursor on cell where changes are to begin.
2. Press / (Menu) .... /
3. Press **F** (File) .... F
4. Press **C** (Combine) C
5. Press **A** (Add) .... A
6. • Press **E** (Entire file) .... E
   to add all numeric data in a file on disk to the current worksheet.
   • Highlight file to be used.

   -OR- OR

   • Press **N** (Named/specified-range) .... N
   to add numeric data in a range on a saved file to the current worksheet.
   • Type range name.
   • **ENTER** .... ↵
   • Highlight file to be used.
7. **ENTER** .... ↵

(continued)

COMBINING FILES (continued)

Subtracting Data

NOTE: • *Subtracts numbers and the results of numeric formulas in a saved worksheet file from numbers and blank cells in the current worksheet..*
• *File/Combine Subtract works with numeric data only.*
• *Numbers are changed from the disk onto the current worksheet at the cursor location.*

1. Place cursor on cell where subtraction is to begin.
2. Press / (Menu) .... [/]
3. Press **F** (File) .... [F]
4. Press **C** (Combine) .... [C]
5. Press **S** (Subtract) .... [S]
6. • Type **E** (Entire file) .... [E]
   to subtract all numeric data in a file on disk from the current worksheet.
   • Highlight file to be used.

   -OR- OR

   • Press **N** (Named/specified-range) .... [N]
   to subtract numeric data in a range in a file on disk from the current worksheet.
   • Type range name.
   • **ENTER** .... [↵]
   • Highlight file to be used.
7. **ENTER** .... [↵]

(continued)

COPYING

NOTE: Copies a cell, a range of cells, or a formula. *See pages 29-32 to create an absolute condition.*

1. Move cursor to the first cell of worksheet to be copied.
2. Press / (Menu) .... [/]
3. Press **C** (Copy) .... [C]
4. Highlight cell or range of cells to be copied FROM.
5. **ENTER** .... [↵]
6. Move cursor to the first cell of worksheet to be copied TO.
7. Type **.** (Period) .... [.]
   to lock in the range.
8. Highlight cell or range of cells to be copied TO.
9. **ENTER** .... [↵]

COPYING A RANGE OF VALUES

NOTE: Copies a range of data, replacing formulas with actual values.

1. Move cursor in first cell of worksheet to be copied.
2. Press / (Menu) .... [/]
3. Press **R** (Range) .... [R]
4. Press **V** (Value) .... [V]
5. Highlight cell or range of cells to be copied FROM.
6. **ENTER** .... [↵]
7. Place cursor on first cell of worksheet to be copied TO.
8. **ENTER** .... [↵]

CREATING A NEW FILE

1. Press / (Menu) .... [/]
2. Press **F** (File) .... [F]
3. Press **N** (New) .... [N]
4. Press **B** (Before) .... [B]

   -OR- OR

5. Press **A** (After) .... [A]
6. Type filename to be created.
7. **ENTER** .... [↵]

DATA PARSE

NOTE: After file is imported, Data/Parse will separate long labels into distinct text and numeric cell entries.

1. Press / (Menu) .... [/]
2. Press **D** (Data)... [D]
3. Press **P** (Parse) .... [P]
4. Press **F** (Format-Line).. [F]
5. • Press **C** (Create) .... [C]
   to insert format line above the cell cursor.
   • Press **I** (Input Column)......................... [I]
   • Highlight the column range that contains a format line and data to be parsed.
   • **ENTER** .... [↵]
   • Press **O** (Output Range)........................ [O]
   • Highlight the address or range name of the first cell in a blank range large enough to hold rows and columns of parsed data.
   • **ENTER** .... [↵]
   • Press **G** (Go)... [G]

   -OR- OR

   • Press **E** (Edit).. [E]
   to edit the format line.
   • Edit format line.
   • **ENTER** .... [↵]

DELETING A FILE

NOTE: Deletes file from disk.

1. Press / (Menu) .... /
2. Press **F** (File) .... F
3. Press **E** (Erase) .... E
4. Select file type to be listed:

   W lists worksheet files .... W

   P lists print files .... P

   G lists graph files .... G

   O lists all other files .... O

5. Type or highlight file name to be deleted.
6. **ENTER** .... ↵
7. Press **Y** (Yes) .... Y
   to confirm file delete.

   NOTE: File cannot be current worksheet.

   -OR- OR

   Press **N** (No) .... N
   to cancel operation.

DELETING FILES (FROM MEMORY)

NOTE: This feature will delete current files from memory but not from disk.

1. Retrieve file to be deleted.
2. Press / (Menu) .... [/]
3. Press **W** (Worksheet) .... [W]
4. Press **D** (Delete) .... [D]
5. Press **F** (File) .... [F]
6. Highlight file to be deleted from memory.
7. **ENTER** .... [↵]

DELETING WORKSHEETS

1. Place cursor on worksheet to be deleted.
2. Press / (Menu) .... [/]
3. Press **W** (Worksheet) .... [W]
4. Press **D** (Delete) .... [D]
5. Press **S** (Sheet) .... [S]
6. **ENTER** .... [↵]
   to delete current sheet.

   -OR- OR

   - Highlight range of worksheets for desired number of worksheets to be deleted.
   - **ENTER** .... [↵]

DRAWING LINES

NOTE: This procedure may be used for repeating any character within a cell.

Horizontal

1. Place cursor in the cell where the horizontal line is to begin.
2. Press \ (Backslash).. \
   to activate the repeat action.
3. Press - (Hyphen) or = (Equal).................... - or =
   or any other desired character.
4. **ENTER** ....
5. To copy the line to another cell or range of cells, use the Copy procedure. (See page 20.)

Vertical

1. Adjust column to desired width. (See pages 13-15.)
2. Place cursor in the cell where the vertical line is to begin.
3. Type **!**.. !
   or any other desired character.
4. **ENTER** ....
5. To copy the line to another cell or range of cells, use the Copy procedure. (See page 20.)

EDITING AN ENTRY

While Typing

1. Press **Backspace** .... Backspace
   to erase characters to the left
   of the cursor.

   -OR- OR

   Press **ESC** .... Esc
   to cancel entire procedure

   -OR- OR

   - Press **F2** (Edit)................................ F2
   - Use cursor keys to correct entry.
   - **ENTER** .... ↵
     to place edited data into worksheet.

After Data Entry

1. Place cursor on cell to be edited.
2. Press **F2** (Edit).. F2
3. Use cursor keys to correct entry.
4. **ENTER** .... ↵
   to place edited data into worksheet.

ENTERING DATA INTO UNPROTECTED CELLS

NOTE: • *May be used for data entry in a "fill-in-the-blanks" entry form.*
• *In order for UNPROTECT to work, Global Protection must be ON.*

1. Press / (Menu) .... [/]
2. Press **R** (Range) .... [R]
3. Press **U** (Unprot) .... [U]
4. Highlight the cell or range of cells where data will be entered or edited.
5. **ENTER** .... [↵]
6. Press / (Menu) .... [/]
7. Press **R** (Range) .... [R]
8. Press **I** (Input) .... [I]
9. Highlight data input range.

   NOTE: Cells unprotected in step 3 constitute the "data input" range.
10. **ENTER** .... [↵]
11. Enter or edit data in unprotected cells.
12. Press **ESC** .... [Esc] to cancel operation.

ENTERING FORMULAS

Using Arithmetic Symbols

1. Place cursor in the cell where answer should appear.

2. Press + (Plus).. [+]
   to put Lotus 1-2-3 into VALUE Mode.

3. Place cursor in first cell of worksheet to be calculated.

   NOTE: The cursor can be moved to another file.

4. Type desired arithmetic symbol:

   + (addition) .... [+]

   - (subtraction)... [-]

   * (multiplication)... [*]

   / (division)... [/]

5. Place cursor in next cell to be calculated. (Repeat steps 4 & 5 **IF** further calculations are necessary.)

To Add a Comment

- Type **!** .... [;]
- Type **;**.. [;]
- Type comment.

6. **ENTER** ....

(continued)

ENTERING FORMULAS (continued)

Using Arithmetic Symbols For Absolute Conditions

1. Follow steps 1-3 on previous page.

2. Press **F4** (Absolute).. F4
   to indicate a no-change condition.

3. Type desired arithmetic symbol:

   + (addition) .... +

   - (subtraction).. -

   * (multiplication).. *

   / (division).. /

4. Place cursor in next cell to be calculated.

5. Press **F4** (Absolute).. F4
   (Repeat steps 4-6 if further calculations are necessary.)

6. **ENTER** .... ↵

Updating Formulas Referring to Data in Other Files

1. Place cursor in the file that has a formula(s) linked to another file.

2. Press / (Menu) .... /

3. Press F (File) .... F

(continued)

ENTERING FORMULAS (continued)

4. Press **A** (Admin) .... A
5. Press **L** (Link-Refresh) L

Using Built-in Statistical Functions

NOTE: See pages 200-213 for Function Descriptions.

1. Place cursor in the cell where the answer should appear.
2. Type @ ("at" symbol) .... @
3. • Type name of desired function:

SUM (addition) .... S U M

SUMPRODUCT (multiplication and addition) .....

S U M P R O D U C T

MAX (maximum) .... M A X

MIN (minimum) .... M I N

COUNT (count) .... C O U N T

AVG (average) .... A V G

STD (population standard deviation) .... S T D

(continued)

ENTERING FORMULAS (continued)

STDS (sample standard deviation) .... S T D S

VAR (variance).............................. V A R

VARS (sample variance) ...... V A R S

- Press **(** (Open Parenthesis).................... (

  OR OR

- Press **F3** (Name).................................. F3
- Highlight statistical function.
- **ENTER**... ↵

4. Type or highlight range to be calculated.
5. Press **)** (Closed Parenthesis)................................)
6. **ENTER** .... ↵

Using Built-In Statistical Functions For Absolute Conditions

1. Follow steps 1-3 on previous page.
2. Press **(** (Open Parenthesis).. (
3. Type or highlight range to be calculated.
4. Press **F4** (Absolute).. F4 to indicate a no change condition.

(continued)

ENTERING FORMULAS (continued)

5. Press **)** (Closed Parenthesis)..)
6. **ENTER** .... ↵

For Lookup Calculations

1. Place cursor in the cell where answer should appear.
2. Press @ ("at" symbol) .... @
3. Type name of desired function:

   VLOOKUP (Vertical Lookup)
   .... V L O O K U P

   HLOOKUP (Horizontal Lookup)
   .... H L O O K U P
4. Press **(** (Open Parenthesis).. (
5. Type cell address of search item.

   -OR-

   Place cursor on cell that contains search item.
6. Press **,** (Comma)... ,
7. Place cursor on the first cell in the table.
8. Press **.** (Period) ....

(continued)

ENTERING FORMULAS (continued)

9. Highlight entire table.

- Press **F4** (Absolute) .... F4 to lock in range.

10. Press **,** (Comma) .... ,

11. Type a number that represents the column or row number of the table where the data to be returned lies.

    NOTE: First column or row in the table is always 0.

12. Press **)** (Closed Parenthesis) ....)

13 **ENTER** .... ↵

For IF (Logical Functions)

1. Place cursor in the cell where the answer should appear.
2. Press **@** ("at" symbol) .... @
3. Type **IF** .... I F
4. Press **(** (Open Parenthesis) .... (
5. Type the condition to be met.
6. Press **,** (Comma) .... ,
7. Type the argument IF the condition is TRUE.
8. Press **,** (Comma) .... ,

(continued)

ENTERING FORMULAS (continued)

9. Type the argument IF the condition is FALSE.

10. Press **)** (Closed Parenthesis).................................... [ )]

11. **ENTER**.. [↵]

EXAMPLE: The IF statement @IF(B3<2000, B3*.03, B*.05) applied to the problem below and entered in cell C3 will compute a 3% commission for sales less than $2,000 and compute a 5% commission when the cell contains a value greater than or equal to $2,000. (The formula should then be copied for the other salespeople.)

	A	B	C
1	SALESPERSON	SALES	COMMISSION
2			EARNED
3	ADAMS	2000	
4	PRESS	1400	
5	HARRIS	3600	
6			
7			
8			
9			
10			

ENTERING SEQUENTIAL NUMBERS IN A RANGE

1. Place cursor in cell where "start" value should begin.
2. Press **/** (Menu) .... [/]
3. Press **D** (Data) .... [D]
4. Press **F** (Fill) .... [F]
5. Highlight range where "fill" data will appear.
6. **ENTER** .... [↵]
7. Type the "start" value.

   NOTE: Lotus 1-2-3 uses zero (0) as the start value if one is not specified.

8. **ENTER** .... [↵]

9 Type the "step" value.
(The increment between each of the values in the range.)

   NOTE: Lotus 1-2-3 uses one (1) as the step value if one is not specified.

10. **ENTER** .... [↵]
11. Type the "stop" value.
(A value that limits the sequence.)

    NOTE: Lotus 1-2-3 uses 8191 as the stop value if one is not specified.

12. **ENTER** .... [↵]

ENTERING VALUES

NOTE: • *The mode indicator must say ready.*
• *The entry cannot be more than 512 characters.*
• *A value entry begins with a number or a numeric symbol: + - @ . (# $*
• *DO NOT include spaces or commas in the entry. (Commas may be included by formatting the cell for currency - See page 41-43.)*
• *When a value is entered, the mode indicator will display VALUE.*
• *Values will* ***always*** *right justify after entry; their alignment* ***cannot*** *be changed.*

1. Place cursor in desired cell.

2. Type value entry.

3. **ENTER** .... ↵

   -OR- OR

   Press cursor arrow key in direction of the next entry .... → ↓ ↑ ←

ERASING

NOTE: If necessary save changes before erasing screen.

The Screen/Worksheet

1. Press / (Menu) .... /
2. Press **W** (Worksheet) .... W
3. Press **E** (Erase) .... E
4. Press **Y** (Yes) .... Y
   - If worksheet has been changed and is not to be saved: Press **Y** .... Y

A Cell or Range of Cells

NOTE: Erased cells can be recovered with UNDO. (See page 151.)

1. Place cursor on cell to be erased.
2. Press / (Menu) .... /
3. Press **R** (Range) .... R
4. Press **E** (Erase) .... E
5. Highlight cell or range of cells to be erased.
6. **ENTER** .... ↵

EXITING LOTUS 1-2-3

To Exit Temporarily

1. Press **/** (Menu) .... /
2. Press **S** (System) .... S
3. Type desired DOS commands or program to run.
4. After running desired program, return to DOS.
5. Type **EXIT** .... E X I T
   to return to LOTUS 1-2-3.
6. **ENTER** .... ↵

To Exit Session

NOTE: Save file or erase worksheet before exiting.

1. Press **/** (Menu) .... /
2. Press **Q** (Quit) .... Q
3. Press **Y** .... Y
   to exit.

   -OR-

   Press **N** .... N
   to return to worksheet.

FINDING FREQUENCY OF DATA DISTRIBUTION

1. Place cursor at the top of an empty column adjacent to the last column of data.

2. Enter desired values to be used for data distribution (in ascending order).

   NOTE: This is referred to as the "bin" range.

3. Press / (Menu) .... [/]

4. Press **D** (Data) .... [D]

5. Press **D** (Distribution) .... [D]

6. Highlight range of values to be calculated in frequency distribution.

7. **ENTER** .... [↵]

8. Highlight "bin" range.

9. **ENTER** .... [↵]

   NOTE: Frequency of values will appear in the column to the right of the bin range.

FIXING/FREEZING TITLES

1. Place cursor one ROW below or one COLUMN to the right of where the freeze is to occur.
2. Press / (Menu) .... /
3. Press **W** (Worksheet) .... W
4. Press **T** (Titles) .... T
5. Select a freeze option:

B (Both)	Freezes rows above cursor and columns to left of cursor	B
H (Horizontal)	Freezes rows above cursor	H
V (Vertical)	Freezes columns to left of cursor	V

Clearing Title Freeze

1. Place cursor one ROW below or one COLUMN to the right of where the unfreeze is to occur.
2. Press / (Menu) .... H
3. Press **W** (Worksheet) .... W
4. Press **T** (Titles) .... T
5. Press **C** (Clear) C

FORMATTING

Local

NOTE: Will affect each cell in a range and override global cell formats.

1. Place cursor in the first cell where the desired format should appear.
2. Press **/** (Menu) .... [/]
3. Press **R** (Range) .... [R]
4. Press **F** (Format) .... [F]
5. Select a desired format:

Key	Format	Description	Keystroke
F	(Fixed)	Displays numbers up to 15 decimal places..........	[F]
S	(Scientific)	Displays numbers up to 15 decimal places in scientific notation..........	[S]
C	(Currency)	Displays currency symbols: dollar signs ($) and commas (,)..........	[C]
,	(Comma)	Displays numbers with commas..........	[,]
G	(General)	Displays negative numbers with a minus sign (-), without commas, & without trailing zeros	[G]

(continued)

FORMATTING (continued)

+ or **-**	Displays numbers as either a plus (+), (-) or (.) symbol, thus creating a horizontal bar graph	**+** or **-**
P (Percent)	Displays numbers with percent symbols, up to 15 decimal places..........	**P**
D (Date)	Displays serial date numbers and (Time) time in various formats	**D**
T (Text)	Displays formulas entered rather than computed values................	**T**
H (Hidden)	Does not display cell contents............................	**H**
O (Other)	Displays cells automatically formatted, with colors, using labels, or in parentheses	**O**
R (Reset)	Resets the range to global cell format...............	**R**

6. Type desired number of decimal places (0-15).

   -OR-

   - Select a desired format (for Date and Time).

(continued)

FORMATTING (continued)

7. **ENTER** for single cell formatting .... ↵

   -OR- OR

   - Highlight the range of cells to be formatted.
   - **ENTER** .... ↵

Global

NOTE: Will affect the entire worksheet.

1. Place cursor anywhere on the worksheet.
2. Press / (Menu) .... /
3. Press **W** (Worksheet) .... W
4. Press **G** (Global) .... G
5. Press **F** (Format) .... F
6. Follow steps 5-6 on previous pages.
7. **ENTER** .... ↵

GRAPHING

Creating an Automatic Graph

NOTE: The leftmost column around the cell pointer becomes the X range and the columns immediately to the right of the first column become the A through F data ranges.

1. Retrieve worksheet from which graph is to be created.
2. Place cursor in first cell of data range of graph.
3. Press **F10** (Graph) F10

*NOTE: To change the data ranges to default to columns or rows, use /**W**orksheet **G**lobal **D**efault **G**raph **C**olumnwise or **R**owwise or /**G**raph **G**roup **C**olumnwise or **R**owwise.*

Creating a Group Graph

NOTE: The Graph Group feature selects all the data ranges for adjacent rows or columns in one step.

1. Retrieve worksheet from which graph is to be created.
2. Place cursor in first cell of data range of graph.
3. Press / (Menu) .... /
4. Press **G** (Graph) .... G
5. Press **G** (Group) .... G

(continued)

GRAPHING (continued)

6. Highlight data range for the graph.

7. **ENTER** .... [↵]

8. Select division of data ranges:

   C (Columnwise).. [C]
   to use columns as data ranges.

   -OR- OR

   R (Rowwise).. [R]
   to use rows as data range.

9. Press **V** (View)... [V]

Creating a Graph

NOTE: The X axis is the horizontal scale.
The Y axis is the vertical scale.

1. Retrieve worksheet from which graph is to be created.

2. Press / (Menu)... [/]

3. Press **G** (Graph).. [G]

4. Press **T** (Type).. [T]

5. Select desired graph type:

   L (Line)... [L]

   B (Bar).. [B]

(continued)

GRAPHING (continued)

X (XY) Shows correlations between two types of numeric data........ X

S (Stacked-Bar).. S

P (Pie) .... P

HLCO (High-Low-Close-Open) Tracks data fluctuations during specific periods. .... H

M (Mixed) Combines line and bars in same graph.......................... M

F (Features).. F

- **V**ertical Draws graph vertically........... V
- **H**orizontal Draws graph horizontally .... H
- **S**tacked Stacks data ranges .... S
- **1**00% Groups data ranges as percentages of total................ 1
- **2**Y-Ranges Sets ranges for second Y-axis 2
- **Y**-Ranges Sets ranges for Y-axis .... Y
- **Q**uit Returns to graph menu.......... Q

6. Press **X**.. X
   to sets X-axis **label** range.

(continued)

GRAPHING (continued)

7. Press . (Period).. [.]
   to lock in the range.
8. Highlight range to be scaled.
9. **ENTER**.. [↵]
10. Press **A**.. [A]
    to set Y-axis data range.

    NOTE: • *"A" is the only data range used in a pie chart.*
    • *Use this data range to represent high values in a HLCO graph.*
    • *Use A-C data ranges to indicate values to be represented as bars and D-F data ranges to indicate values to be represented as lines in a mixed graph.*
11. Press . (Period).. [.]
    to lock in the range.
12. Highlight range to be scaled.
13. **ENTER**.. [↵]

(continued)

Setting Additional Data Ranges:

14. • Press **B** .... [B]
   to set second Y-Axis data range
   or to set pie chart shading values.

   NOTE: Use this data range to represent low values in a HLCO graph, or to indicate the values for controlling hatch patterns or colors in a pie chart, or for exploding slices of the pie in a pie chart.

   • Press **C** .... [C]
   to set third Y-axis data range.

   NOTE: Use this data range to represent closing values in a HLCO graph.

   • Press **D** .... [D]
   to set fourth data range.

   NOTE: Use this data range to represent opening values in a HLCO graph.

   • Press **E** .... [E]
   to set fifth data range.

   • Press **F** .... [F]
   to set sixth data range.

15. Press **.** (Period) .... [.]
   to lock in the range.

16. Highlight range to be scaled.

17. **ENTER** .... [↵]

(continued)

GRAPHING OPTIONS - Enhancing a Graph

Creating a Legend

NOTE: • *If already working in a graphing submenu, steps 1 and 2 below need not be repeated.*
• *The legend is a caption which explains each data range in a graph or the segments of a pie chart.*

1. Press / (Menu).. [/]
2. Press **G** (Graph).. [G]
3. Press **O** (Options).. [O]
4. Press **L** (Legend).. [L]
5. Press **A** .... [A]
   to name legend for first data range.
6. Type name for first legend.
7. **ENTER**.. [↵]

To Name Additional Legends:

8. Press **L** (Legend) .... [L]
   - Press **B** .... [B]
     to name legend for second data range.

     -Type legend name.

     -**ENTER**.. [↵]

(continued)

GRAPHING OPTIONS (continued)

- Press **C** C
  to name legend for third data range.

  -Type legend name.

  -ENTER .... ↵

- Press **D** .... D
  to name legend for fourth data range.

  -Type legend name.

  -ENTER .... ↵
  to name legend for fifth data range.

  -Type legend name.

  -ENTER .... ↵

- Press **F** .... F
  to name legend for sixth data range.

  -Type legend name.

  -ENTER .... ↵

- Press **R** (Range) .... R
  to indicate range containing legends for all data ranges.

  -Type legend range.

  -ENTER .... ↵

(continued)

GRAPHING OPTIONS (continued)

Creating Titles

NOTE: If already working in a graphing submenu, steps 1 and 2 below need not be repeated.

1. Press / (Menu) .... /
2. Press **G** (Graph) .... G
3. Press **O** (Options) .... O
4. Press **T** (Titles) .... T
5. Press **F** (First) .... F
6. Type a title or heading.
7. **ENTER** .... ↵

If a subtitle is desired:

8. Repeat steps 4-7. At step 5, Press **S** (Second) .... S

To assign an X-Axis title:

9. Repeat steps 4-7. At step 5, Press **X** (X-Axis) X

To assign a Y-Axis title:

10. Repeat steps 4-7. At step 5, Press **Y** (Y-Axis) .... Y

(continued)

GRAPHING OPTIONS (continued)

To assign the second Y-axis title:

11. Repeat steps 4-7. At step 5,
Press **2** (2Y-Axis) 2

To assign a footnote:

12. Repeat steps 4-7. At step 5,
Press **N** (Note) .... N

To assign a second line to the footnote:

13. Repeat steps 4-7. At step 5,
Press **O** (Other-Note) .... O

Creating Data Labels

NOTE: • *If already working in the graphing submenu, steps 1 and 2 below need not be repeated.*
• *A data label indicates values plotted on a bar or line graph and usually appears at the top of each bar or at the plotted point on a line graph.*

1 Press / (Menu) .... /

2. Press **G** (Graph) .... G

3. Press **O** (Options) .... O

4. Press **D** (Data-Labels) .... D

(continued)

GRAPHING OPTIONS (continued)

5. Select a range to be labeled:

   A .... A

   B .... B

   C C

   D .... D

   E .... E

   F .... F

   G (Group) Assigns all data labels .... G

   -OR- OR

   Q (Quit) Cancels operation........................ Q

6. Highlight range containing the labels.

7. **ENTER**.. ↵

8. Select a label alignment option:

   C (Center).. C

   L (Left) L

   A (Above)... A

   R (Right) .... R

   B (Below) .... B

(continued)

GRAPHING OPTIONS (continued)

If **G** (Group) was selected above, select one of the following label alignment options:

C (Columnwise) .... [C]
to use columns as data ranges.

-OR- OR

R (Rowwise) .... [R]
to use rows as data ranges.

Then,
Select a label alignment option:

-**C**enter .... [C]

-**L**eft.. [L]

-**A**bove.. [A]

-**R**ight.. [R]

-**B**elow... [B]

9. Press **Q** (Quit)... [Q]

(continued)

GRAPHING OPTIONS (continued)

Creating a Graph Window

NOTE: • *A graph window simultaneously displays the worksheet and its graph. Any changes to the graph's data in the worksheet is automatically reflected in the graph.*
• *A blank graph window will display if proper graphics monitor is unavailable.*

1. Place cursor in column E.
2. Press / (Menu).. /
3. Press **W** (Worksheet) .... W
4. Press **W** (Window) .... W
5. Press **G** (Graph).. G

NOTE: The graph will appear beginning in column E.

6. Edit the data in the worksheet and the graph will update with the changes.

Closing a Graph Window

1. Press / (Menu).. /
2. Press **W** (Worksheet) .... W
3. Press **W** (Window) .... W
4. Press **C** (Clear).. C

(continued)

GRAPHING OPTIONS (continued)

Exploding a Pie Chart/Specifying a Color or Hatch Pattern

NOTE: • *If already working in the graphing submenu, steps 1 and 2 below need not be repeated.*
• *Use this option to separate an individual slice from the whole pie and/or to indicate a different hatch pattern or color for specific or all slices of the pie.*

1. Enter a number from 1-8 in each cell on a blank area of the spreadsheet to indicate a different hatch pattern (for the B data range). To explode a piece of the pie, add 100 to the B data range values. For example, if you wanted to explode piece 2, the second value in the B data range would be indicated as 102. Each number must equal the number of slices in the pie. The number in the first cell indicates the hatch pattern for the pie slice that corresponds to the first value in the A data range.
2. Press **/** (Menu)........ [/]
3. Press **G** (Graph)........ [G]
4. Press **B**........ [B]
5. Press **.** (Period)........ [.]
   to lock in the range.
6. Highlight the B data range.

(continued)

GRAPHING OPTIONS (continued)

7. **ENTER**.. [↵]
8. Press **V** (View).. [V]
9. Press **Q** (Quit).. [Q]

Modifying a Line, XY or Mixed Graph

NOTE: • *If already working in the graphing submenu, steps 1 and 2 below need not be repeated.*
• *Use this feature to connect data points with lines or mark them with symbols, convert a line graph to an area graph, stack an XY graph.*

1. Press **/** (Menu).. [/]
2. Press **G** (Graph).. [G]
3. Press **O** (Options).. [O]
4. Press **F** (Format).. [F]
5. Select a range to format:

   Graph .... [G]
   to format all ranges.

   A .... [A]

   B .... [B]

   C .... [C]

(continued)

GRAPHING OPTIONS (continued)

D .... D

E .... E

F .... F

6. Select a modify option:

L (Lines)	Connects data points with lines	L
S (Symbols)	Displays a symbol at each data point	S
B (Both)	Displays a symbol at each data point and connect data points with lines	B
N (Neither)	Displays neither lines nor symbols and hide data points	N
A (Area)	Fills area under lines..........	A

7. Press **Q** (Quit) .... Q

8. Press **Q** (Quit) .... Q

9. Press **V** (View) V

10. Press **Q** (Quit) .... Q

(continued)

GRAPHING OPTIONS (continued)

Modifying Graph Grids

NOTE: • *If already working in the graphing submenu, steps 1 and 2 below need not be repeated.*
• *Use this feature to change the display of grid lines or remove them completely.*

1. Press / (Menu).. [/]
2. Press **G** (Graph).. [G]
3. Press **O** (Options).. [O]
4. Press **G** (Grid).. [G]
5. Select a grid option:

H (Horizontal)	Creates grid lines across graph......................	[H]
V (Vertical)	Creates grid lines up/down graph..................	[V]
B (Both)	Creates grid lines across and up/down graph...........	[B]
C (Clear)	Clears all grid lines...........	[C]
Y (Y-axis)	Selects Y-axis for grids across graph...........	[Y]

(continued)

Then, select the Y-axis:

-**Y** (first) .... Y

-**2**Y (second) 2

-**B**oth (both axes) .... B

6. Press **Q** (Quit) .... Q

Scaling an Axis

NOTE: • If already working in the graphing submenu, steps 1 and 2 below need not be repeated.
• Use this feature to change the display of grid lines or remove them completely.

1. Press **/** (Menu) .... /
2. Press **G** (Graph) .... G
3. Press **O** (Options) .... O
4. Press **S** (Scale) .... S
5. Select axis to be scaled:

Y (Y-Scale) .... Y

-OR- OR

X (X-Scale) X

-OR- OR

(continued)

GRAPHING OPTIONS (continued)

S (Skip) .... S
to display every nth cell in X range.

-OR- OR

2 (2Y-Sale) 2
to display second Y-axis scaling.

If Y, X or 2Y-scale were selected:

6. Select a scaling option:

A (Automatic) .... A

M (Manual) .... M

L (Lower) L

-Type lower limit.

-ENTER .... ↵

U (Upper) .... U

-Type upper limit.

-ENTER .... ↵

F (Format) .... F

-Select a format option:

-Fixed .... F

-Sci .... S

(continued)

GRAPHING OPTIONS (continued)

- -**C**urrency C
- -, (comma) .... ,
- -**G**eneral .... G
- -**+/-** (plus or minus) ...... + or -
- -**P**ercent .... P
- -**D**ate .... D
- -**T**ext .... T
- -**H**idden .... H

I (Indicator) I

Select an indicator option:

- -**Y**es .... Y
- -**N**one .... N
- -**M**anual .... M

T (Type) .... T

- -**S**tandard .... S

  -OR- OR

- -**L**ogarithmic L

E (Exponent) .... E

- -**A**utomatic .... A

(continued)

GRAPHING OPTIONS (continued)

-OR- OR

-**M**anual.................................... M

W (Width) .... W

-**A**utomatic.................................. A

-OR- OR

-**M**anual.................................... M

Q (Quit) .... Q

7. Press **Q** (Quit).. Q

Changing Colors

NOTE: • If already in the graphing submenu, steps 1 and 2 below need not be repeated.
• Use this feature to change the colors and hide the A-F data ranges.

1. Press **/** (Menu).. /
2. Press **G** (Graph).. G
3. Press **O** (Option).. O
4. Press **A** (Advanced).. A
5. Press **C** (Colors) C

(continued)

GRAPHING OPTIONS (continued)

6. Select a data range:

A .... A

B .... B

C C

D .... D

E .... E

F .... F

7. Select a color option:

1 1

2 2

3 3

4 4

5 5

6 6

7 7

8 8

H (Hide) .... H
to hide data range.

R (Range) .... R
to set color or hide data range.

(continued)

GRAPHING OPTIONS (continued)

If **R** (Range) was selected above, then:

-Highlight range for color change.

-ENTER.. [↵]

8. Repeat steps 6-8 to set colors for other data ranges.

Changing Hatch Patterns

NOTE: • *If already in the graphing submenu, steps 1 and 2 below need not be repeated.*
• *Use this to change the hatch patterns for the A-F data ranges.*

1. Press / (Menu).. [/]
2. Press **G** (Graph).. [G]
3. Press **O** (Option).. [O]
4. Press **A** (Advanced).. [A]
5. Press **H** (Hatches).. [H]
6. Select a data range:

A.. [A]

B.. [B]

C.. [C]

D.. [D]

(continued)

GRAPHING OPTIONS (continued)

E .... [E]

F .... [F]

7. Select a color option:

1 .... [1]

2 .... [2]

3 .... [3]

4 .... [4]

5 .... [5]

6 .... [6]

7 .... [7]

8 .... [8]

R (Range) .... [R]
to set color or hide data range.

If **R** (Range) was selected above, then:

-Highlight range for color change.

-ENTER .... [↵]

8. Repeat steps 6-8 to set colors for other data ranges.

(continued)

GRAPHING OPTIONS (continued)

Changing Colors, Fonts, and Sizes for Graph Text

NOTE: If already in the graphing submenu, steps 1 and 2 below need not be repeated.

1. Press / (Menu).. [/]
2. Press **G** (Graph).. [G]
3. Press **O** (Option).. [O]
4. Press **A** (Advanced).. [A]
5. Press **T** (Text).. [T]
6. Select a graph-text group:

   F (First) Sets text attributes for first graph title.................... [F]

   S (Second) Sets text attributes for second graph title, axis titles, and legends.......................... [S]

   T (Third) Sets text attributes for scale indicators, axis and data labels, and footnotes........ [T]

7. Select the text attribute to be changed:

   C (Color).. [C]

   -Select a color option:

   -1.. [1]

(continued)

GRAPHING OPTIONS (continued)

- -2 2
- -3 3
- -4 4
- -5 5
- -6 6
- -7 7
- -8 8
- -H (Hide) .... H

F (Font) .... F

- -Select a font option:
- -1 1
- -2 2
- -3 3
- -4 4
- -5 5
- -6 6
- -7 7
- -8 8

(continued)

GRAPHING OPTIONS (continued)

-**D** (Default).. D

S (Size) .... S

-Select a size option:

-**1**.. 1

-**2**.. 2

-**3**.. 3

-**4**.. 4

-**5**.. 5

-**6**.. 6

-**7**.. 7

-**8**.. 8

-**D** (Default).. D

(continued)

GRAPHING OPTIONS (continued)

Cancelling Graph Settings

1. Press **/** (Menu) .... [/]
2. Press **G** (Graph) .... [G]
3. Press **R** (Reset) .... [R]
4. Select a reset option:

G (Graph)	Resets all graph settings	[G]
X	Resets X-data range.	[X]
A-F	Resets A-F data range(s)	[A]-[F]
R (Range)	Resets all data range settings	[R]
O (Options)	Resets all options settings	[O]
Q (Quit)	To return to graph menu	[Q]

Viewing Graphs

NOTE: If already working in the graphing submenu, steps 1 and 2 below need not be repeated.

Procedure 1

1. Press **/** (Menu) .... [/]

(continued)

GRAPHING OPTIONS (continued)

2. Press **G** (Graph) .... G
3. Press **V** (View) V

Procedure II

While in READY MODE :

- Press **F10** (Graph Key) F10

Saving Graphs (for other applications)

NOTE: • If already in the graphing submenu, steps 1 and 2 below need not be repeated.
*• Graphs can be saved as metafiles (.CGM) or Lotus 1- 2-3 files (.PIC). To change the default format, use /**W**orksheet **G**lobal **D**efault **G**raph **M**etafile (.CGM) or PIC.*

1. Press **/** (Menu) .... /
2. Press **G** (Graph) .... G
3. Press **S** (Save) .... S
4. Type name of graph to be saved.
5. **ENTER** .... ↵

(continued)

GRAPHING OPTIONS (continued)

Saving Graphs (for recall)

NOTE: • *If already working in the graphing submenu, steps 1 and 2 below need not be repeated.*
• *The graphs are only associated with the current file.*

1. Press / (Menu) .... [/]
2. Press **G** (Graph) .... [G]
3. Press **N** (Name) .... [N]
4. Press **C** (Create) .... [C]
5. **ENTER** .... [↵]
6. Type a graph name.
7. **ENTER** .... [↵]

Using Graphs (for recall)

NOTE: • *If already in the graphing submenu, steps 1 and 2 below need not be repeated.*
• *The graphs are only available with the current file.*

1. Press / (Menu) .... [/]
2. Press **G** (Graph) .... [G]
3. Press **N** (Name) .... [N]

(continued)

GRAPHING OPTIONS (continued)

4. Press **U** (Use) .... [U]
5. Highlight a graph name.
6. **ENTER** .... [↵]

Deleting a Graph (for recall)

NOTE: • If already in the graphing submenu, steps 1 and 2 below need not be repeated.
• The graphs are only available with the current file.

1. Press / (Menu) .... [/]
2. Press **G** (Graph) .... [G]
3. Press **N** (Name) .... [N]
4. Press **D** (Delete) .... [D]
5. Highlight a graph name.
6. **ENTER** .... [↵]

Deleting All Graphs (for recall)

NOTE: • If already in the graphing submenu, steps 1 and 2 below need not be repeated.
• The graphs are only available with the current file.

1. Press / (Menu) .... [/]

(continued)

GRAPHING OPTIONS (continued)

2. Press **G** (Graph) .... G
3. Press **N** (Name) .... N
4. Press **R** (Reset) .... R

Listing Graphs (Graphs / Name Table)

NOTE: Will create an alphabetical list of created graphs, graph types and titles associated with the file.

1. Place cursor in a cell in an available section of the worksheet.
2. Press **/** (Menu) .... /
3. Press **G** (Graph) .... G
4. Press **N** (Name) .... N
5. Press **T** (Table) .... T
6. Highlight cell to begin list.
7. **ENTER** .... ↵

(continued)

GRAPHING OPTIONS (continued)

Printing Graphs

1. Press / (Menu) .... /
2. Press **P** (Print) .... P
3. Press **P** (Printer) .... P
4. Press **I** (Image) I
5. Press **C** (Current) C

   -OR- OR

   - Press **N** (Named-Graph) .... N
   - Highlight a graph to be printed.
   - **ENTER** .... ↵
6. Press **A** (Align) .... A
7. Press **G** (Go) .... G
8. Press **Q** (Quit) .... Q

GROUP MODE

NOTE: This feature enables all worksheets in a file to take on the worksheet settings of current worksheet. Changes made to any worksheet are mimicked in others.

1. Press / (Menu) .... /
2. Press **W** (Worksheet) .... W
3. Press **G** (Global) .... G
4. Press **G** (Group) .... G
5. Press **E** (Enable) .... E

Turning Group Mode Off

1. Press / (Menu) .... /
2. Press **W** (Worksheet) .... W
3. Press **G** (Global) .... G
4. Press **G** (Group) .... G
5. Press **D** (Disenable) .... D

HELP

1. Press **F1** (Help).. F1

Context Selective Help

1. Select menu command.
2. Press **F1** (Help).. F1

HIDING COLUMNS

NOTE: Hides selected columns without erasing data. Formulas in hidden columns continue to work correctly.

1. Press / (Menu) .... /
2. Press **W** (Worksheet) .... W
3. Press **C** (Column) C
4. Press **H** (Hide) .... H
5. Highlight range of columns to be hidden.
6. **ENTER** .... ↵

Redisplaying Hidden Columns

1. Press / (Menu) .... /
2. Press **W** (Worksheet) .... W
3. Press **C** (Column) C
4. Press **D** (Display) .... D
5. Highlight range of columns to be redisplayed.
6. **ENTER** .... ↵

HIGHLIGHTING RANGES

1. Place cursor in first cell in the range to be highlighted.

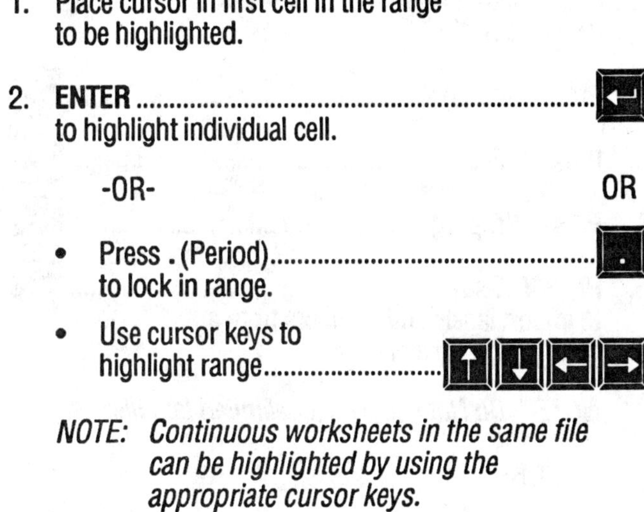

2. ENTER ....
   to highlight individual cell.

   -OR- OR

   - Press . (Period)..
     to lock in range.
   - Use cursor keys to highlight range..........................

   NOTE: Continuous worksheets in the same file can be highlighted by using the appropriate cursor keys.

3. ENTER ....

IMPORTING A FILE

1. Place cursor in cell where imported data is to begin.
2. Press / (Menu) .... /
3. Press **F** (File) .... F
4. Press **I** (Import) I
5. Press **T** (Text) .... T
   to import labels and numbers from a nondelimited text file.

   NOTE: Do Not use with a delimited text file.

   -OR- OR

   Press **N** (Numbers) .... N
   to import only numbers from a nondelimited text file or to import numbers and labels from a delimited text file.
6. Type name of file to be imported.
7. **ENTER** .... ↵

   NOTE: To calculate imported data, it is necessary to use the Data/Parse procedure to place data in cells. *(See page 22.)*

INSERTING / DELETING COLUMNS AND ROWS

Columns

1. Place cursor in the column where the insertion or deletion is to occur.

2. Press **/** (Menu) .... /

3. Press **W** (Worksheet) .... W

4. Press **I** (Insert) I

   -OR- OR

   Press **D** (Delete) .... D

5. Press **C** (Column) C

   -OR- OR

   Press **R** (Row) .... R

6. **ENTER** .... ↵
   to insert or delete **one** column or row.

   -OR- OR

   - Highlight across (for column) or down (for row) for desired number of columns or rows to be inserted or deleted.
   - **ENTER** .... ↵

INSERTING PAGE BREAK

NOTE: • *Will insert desired page breaks in printed worksheets.*
• *DO NOT enter data in the row where page break marker (: :) appears.*

1. Place cursor in row where page break is desired.
2. Press / (Menu) .... /
3. Press **W** (Worksheet) .... W
4. Press **P** (Page) .... P

To Remove Page Break

1. Place cursor in any cell in the row where page break marker appears.
2. Press / (Menu) .... /
3. Press **W** (Worksheet) .... W
4. Press **D** (Delete) .... D
5. Press **R** (Row) .... R
6. **ENTER** .... ↵

INSERTING WORKSHEETS

1. Place cursor in worksheet before or after new worksheet to be inserted.
2. Press / (Menu) .... /
3. Press **W** (Worksheet).................................... W
4. Press **I** (Insert) I
5. Press **S** (Sheet) .... S
6. Press **B** (Before).................................... B

   -OR- OR

   Press **A** (After).................................... A

7. Type the number of worksheets to be inserted. ....**Option**

   NOTE: The total number of active worksheets cannot be more than 256.

8. **ENTER** .... ↵

JUSTIFYING LABELS
(In a Range)

NOTE: • *Paragraphs may be created from columns of labels to fit into a specific width.*
• *Continuous text will justify until a non-label entry is reached.*

1. Press / (Menu) .... [/]
2. Press **R** (Range).. [R]
3. Press **J** (Justify) .... [J]
4. Highlight the range to receive justified text.
5. **ENTER** .... [↵]

LABELS

ENTERING LABELS

NOTE: • *The mode indicator must say READY.*
• *The entry cannot be more than 240 characters.*
• *When a label is longer than the cell's column width, the text will continue into the next cell if it is blank; otherwise, the entry will be truncated.*

Alphabetic

NOTE: Alphabetic labels will automatically left justify after entry. To center, right justify, or fill the cell with a character, see ALIGNING LABELS section on next page.

1. Place cursor in desired cell.

2. Type label text.

3. **ENTER** .... ↵

   -OR- OR

   Press cursor arrow key in direction of next entry .... ↓ → ↑ ←

LABELS (continued)

Numeric

NOTE: Numeric labels ***will not*** *calculate.*

1. Place cursor in desired cell.
2. Type an apostrophe (label prefix)............................ 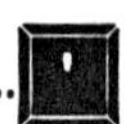

   NOTE: Using an apostrophe as a label prefix will left justify the numeric label and will indicate that the entry is not a value.

3. Type label text.
4. **ENTER** ....

   -OR- OR

   Press cursor arrow key in direction of the next entry. .... 

Aligning Labels (right, center or fill the cell)

Before cell entry

1. Place cursor in desired cell.
2. Type a label prefix option:

   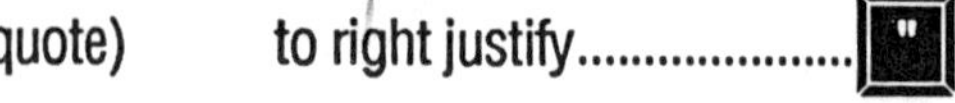

   " (quote) to right justify......................

   ^ (caret) to center..............................

   \ (backslash) to repeat a character to fill the cell.......................

(continued)

LABELS (continued)

3. Type label text.

4. **ENTER** .... ↵

   -OR-   OR

   Press a cursor arrow key in the direction of the next entry .... ↓ → ↑ ←

After cell entry

1. Place cursor in desired cell.
2. Type **/** (Menu) .... /
3. Type **R** (Range) .... R
4 Type **L** (Label).. L
5. Select desired alignment option:

   L (Left) L

   R (Right) .... R

   C (Center)....................................... C

6. **ENTER** (for single-cell alignment).......................... ↵

   -OR-   OR

   - Highlight range of cells to be aligned.
   - **ENTER**.. ↵

LISTING FILES

NOTE: Lists files in the current directory.

1. Press / (Menu) .... /
2. Press **F** (File) .... F
3. Press **L** (List) L
4. Select a file type option:

   W lists worksheet files .... W

   P lists print files .... P

   G lists graph files .... G

   O lists all files .... O

   A lists files in memory .... A

   L lists all files linked to current worksheet by formula references L

Listing Files in a Different Drive/Directory:

5. Press **ESC** .... Esc
6. Press **ESC** .... Esc
7. Type new drive and/or directory.
8. Type a filename (with extension) to list.
9. **ENTER** .... ↵

MACROS

Creating a Macro with the Record Feature

NOTE: • *Macros can be created through the Record Feature by performing the task to be automated.*
• *The record feature will not allow more than 512 bytes (units of characters).*

1. Place cursor in cell where macro task will be recorded.
2. Press **Alt + F2** (Record) .... Alt + F2
3. Press **E** (Erase) .... E
4. Type keystrokes to perform task to be recorded.
5. Press **Alt + F2** (Record) .... Alt + F2
6. Press **C** (Copy) C
7. Place cursor at beginning or end of keystrokes to be copied.
8. Press **TAB** .... Tab
9. Highlight the remaining keys.
10. **ENTER** .... ↵
11. Place cursor in location for recorded keystroke commands.
12. **ENTER** .... ↵

(continued)

Playing a Macro Created with the Record Feature

NOTE: The record feature will not allow more than 512 bytes (units of characters).

1. Place cursor in cell where macro task will be recorded.
2. Press **Alt + F2** (Record) .... Alt + F2
3. Press **E** (Erase) .... E
4. Type keystrokes to perform task to be recorded.
5. Press **Alt + F2** (Record) .... Alt + F2
6. Press **P** (Play) .... P
7. Place cursor at beginning or end of keystrokes to be replayed.
8. Press **TAB** .... Tab
9. Highlight the remaining keys.
10. **ENTER** .... ↵

(continued)

MACROS (continued)

Naming a Macro

1. Press **/** (Menu) .... [/]
2. Press **R** (Range)... [R]
3. Press **N** (Name)... [N]
4. Press **C** (Create) .... [C]
5. Type macro name (as the range name) up to 15 characters.

   NOTE: A macro may be named with a \ (backslash) followed by a letter, e.g.: W.

6. Highlight first cell of the macro as the range to name.

Running a Macro

If macro was named with a \ (backslash) and a single letter:

1. Press **Alt + letter**....................................... [Alt] + **letter**

   If macro was named with characters (or a \ [backslash] and a single letter):

1. Press **Alt + F3** (Run) .... [Alt] + [F3] to display a menu of range names.
2. Highlight macro range name address.
3. **ENTER**... [↵]

(continued)

Debugging a Macro

1. Press **Alt + F2** (Step)................................ Alt + F2
   to turn STEP mode on.

2. Press **S** (Step).. S

3. Depending how macro was named:

   Press **Alt + letter** .... Alt +letter

   -OR- OR

   - Press **Alt + F3** (Run)............ Alt + F3
     to start running the macro.

   - Highlight macro name.

   - **ENTER** .... ↵

4. Press **SPACEBAR** .... Space
   to execute the first macro instruction.

   NOTE: Repeat step 4 as many times as necessary to find macro error.

5. Press **CTRL + BREAK** .... Ctrl + Break
   to end the macro.

6. Press **ESC**.. Esc

7. Press **Alt + F2** (Step).................................. Alt + F2
   to turn STEP mode off.

8. Press **S** (Step).. S

(continued)

MACROS (continued)

To Edit the Macro:

9. Place cursor in macro range.
10. Press **F2** (Edit) F2
11. Edit macro.
12. **ENTER** .... ↵
13. Run the macro again.

Saving a Macro

1. Press / (Menu) .... /
2. Press **F** (File) .... F
3. Press **S** (Save) .... S
4. Type file name.

   NOTE: The macro will be saved as part of the worksheet.

5. **ENTER** .... ↵

MOVING

NOTE: Moves a cell or range of cells (including Columns and Rows) to a blank area.

1. Place cursor on first cell of worksheet to be moved.
2. Press / (Menu).. /
3. Press **M** (Move).. M
4. Highlight cell or range of cells to be moved FROM.
5. **ENTER**.. ↵
6. Place cursor on first cell of worksheet in the range to be moved TO.
7. **ENTER**.. ↵

MOVING THE CELL CURSOR

NOTE: The actions below may be used in the READY and POINT mode.

To Move within a worksheet:

Right (one cell) .... →

Left (one cell) .... ←

Down (one cell) .... ↓

Up (one cell) .... ↑

Screen Page Down .... PgUp

Screen Page Up .... PgDn

Screen Page Right
(in READY and POINT modes) .... Ctrl + → or Tab

Screen Page Left
(in READY and
POINT modes) .... Ctrl + ← or Shift + Tab

Directly to a Cell

1. Press **F5** (GOTO) F5
2. Type cell address.
3. **ENTER** .... ↵

Home (A1) Position .... Home

Left Edge of a List .... End + ←

Right Edge of a List .... End + →

Top of a List .... End + ↑

(continued)

MOVING THE CELL CURSOR (continued)

Bottom of a List.. End + ↓

NOTE: The actions below may be used in the READY and POINT modes.

To move between worksheets:

End Next Worksheet.................. End, Ctrl + PgUp

End Previous Worksheet.......... End, Ctrl + PgDn

First Cell (A:A1)................................. Ctrl + Home

First File
(last highlighted cell).............. Ctrl + End, Home

Last Cell
(active area of current file)..... End, Ctrl + Home

Last File (cell last highlighted)... Ctrl + End, End

Next File (cell
last highlighted).......... Ctrl + End, Ctrl + PgUp

Next Worksheet.................................. Ctrl + PgUp

Previous File (cell
last highlighted).......... Ctrl + End, Ctrl + PgDn

Previous Worksheet............................ Ctrl + PgDn

NOTE:
- *End Next/Previous Worksheet moves backward/forward to the next worksheet that has data and has a blank cell in front or behind it.*
- *In Edit mode, Next Sheet and Previous Sheet completes editing.*

OPENING A NEW FILE

1. Press **/** (Menu) .... /
2. Press **F** (File) .... F
3. Press **O** (Open) .... O
4. Press **B** (Before) .... B

   -OR- OR

   Press **A** (After) .... A
5. Type or highlight filename.
6. **ENTER** .... ↵

PRINTING

NOTE: LOTUS 1-2-3 prints in the background. The worksheet can be edited while it is printing.

1. Place cursor on first cell to be printed.
2. Press / (Menu) .... /
3. Press **P** (Print) .... P
4. Press **P** (Printer) .... P
5. Press **R** (Range) .... R
6. Press **.** (Period) to lock in the range ....
7. Highlight range to be printed.

   NOTE: A range from multiple worksheets can be selected by typing a semi-colon between ranges, e.g.: A:A1..A:B2, B:E1..F6.

8. **ENTER** .... ↵
9. Press **A** (Align) .... A
10. Press **G** (Go) .... G
11. Press **Q** (Quit) .... Q

(continued)

A Worksheet (or Selected Range to a Text File on Disk

NOTE: Creates an ASCII file which may be used in word processing.

1. Place cursor on first cell to be printed.
2. Press / (Menu) .... /
3. Press **P** (Print) .... P
4. Press **F** (File) .... F
5. Type name of text file to be created.

   NOTE: A .PRN extension will automatically be assigned to the file.

6. **ENTER** .... ↵
7. Press **R** (Range) .... R
8. Highlight range to be printed to disk.
9. **ENTER** .... ↵

10 Press **O** (Options) .... O

11. Press **M** (Margins) .... M

12 Press **N** (None) .... N
to reset margins to 0.

13. Press **O** (Other) .... O

(continued)

14. Press **U** (unformatted) .... U
    to delete headers, footers, and page breaks.

15. Press **ESC** .... Esc

16. Press **A** (Align) .... A

17. Press **G** (Go).. G

18. Press **Q** (Quit).. Q

A Worksheet in Compressed Print

NOTE: Compressed print may also be accomplished through the WYSIWYG add-in. See page 161 to attach add-in; see pages 162-163 to compress print.

1. Place cursor on first cell to be printed.

2. Press **/** (Menu) .... /

3. Press **P** (Print).. P

4. Press **P** (Printer).. P

5. Press **R** (Range).. R

6. Press **.** (period) to lock in the range........................ .

7. Highlight range to be printed.

8. **ENTER** .... ↵

(continued)

PRINTING (continued)

9. Press **O** (Options).. O
10. Press **M** (Margins).. M
11. Press **R** (Right).. R
12. Type 132 (for standard
    80-column printer).. 1 3 2

    -OR- OR

    Type 240 (for a wide-column printer)...... 2 4 0
13. **ENTER**.. ↵
14. Press **S** (Setup).. S
15. Press \ (Backslash).. \
16. Type Setup String (refer to printer manual
    for appropriate code)..**Option**

    NOTE: \015 may be used for EPSON printers.
17. **ENTER**.. ↵
18. Press **ESC**.. Esc
19. Press **A** (Align).. A
20. Press **G** (Go).. G
21. Press **Q** (Quit).. Q

(continued)

A Worksheet with Borders

NOTE:
- *Will print selected rows or columns on every page.*
- *Border rows and columns must correspond to a print range.*
- *Do not include rows and columns as borders that were included in the print range.*

NOTE: Borders may be added or removed through the WYSIWYG add-in. See page 161 to attach add-in; see pages 191-193 to add/remove borders.

1. Place cursor on first cell to be included in the border.
2. Press / (Menu) .... /
3. Press **P** (Print).................... P
4. Press **P** (Printer).................... P
5. Press **O** (Options).................... O
6. Press **B** (Borders).................... B
7. Select a border option:

   C (Columns) Prints vertical headings on left side of each page.... C

   R (Rows) Prints horizontal headings across top of each page..... R

(continued)

PRINTING (continued)

F (Frame) Prints worksheet frame with print range........ F

N (No-Frame) Prints worksheet frame without print range .... N

- If columns or border were selected:

Highlight column or row to be used as border.

ENTER........ ↵

8. Press **ESC**........ Esc
9. Press **A** (Align)........ A
10. Press **G** (Go)........ G
11. Press **Q** (Quit)........ Q

(continued)

A Worksheet with Adjusted Margins

NOTE Adjusting margins on the worksheet may be accomplished through the WYSIWYG add-in. See page 161 to attach add-in; see pages 191-192 to adjust margins.

NOTE: Overrides default margins and sets left, right, top and bottom margins.

1. Press / (Menu) .... [/]
2. Press **P** (Print) .... [P]
3. Press **P** (Printer) .... [P]
4. Press **O** (Options) .... [O]
5. Press **M** (Margins) .... [M]
6. Select a margin option:

L (Left)	Sets margins from left edge from 0-1000 characters .... [L]
R (Right)	Sets margins from left edge (to right) from 0-1000 characters .... [R]
B (Bottom)	Sets margins from Bottom edge from 0-240 lines .... [B]

(continued)

PRINTING (continued)

T (Top) — Sets margins from top edge from 0-240 lines .... T

N (None) — Clears current margins settings, resets top, left and bottom margins to 0, and right margin to 240..... N

7. **ENTER** .... ↵
   to accept margin setting.

   -OR- OR

   - Type desired left, right, bottom or top margin number ....**Option**
   - **ENTER**.. ↵

8. Repeat steps 5-7 for each change to be made.
9. Press **ESC** .... Esc
10. Press **A** (Align) .... A
11. Press **G** (Go).. G
12. Press **Q** (Quit).. Q

(continued)

A Worksheet with Headers and/or Footers

NOTE • Header and footer text may be centered, left or right-justified by preceding the header/footer entry with vertical bars as follows:

centered: ¦ (one vertical bar)
right-justified: ¦¦ (two vertical bars)
left-justified: None

• Lotus 1-2-3 will not print a footer on last page of print run unless / P P P is entered after print job.

1. Place cursor on first cell of the range to be printed.
2. Press **/** (Menu) .... /
3. Press **P** (Print).. P
4. Press **P** (Printer).. P
5. Press **O** (Options).. O
6. Press **H** (Header) .... H

   -OR- OR

   Press **F** (Footer)... F
7. • Type header or footer text.

   -OR-

   • Type \ (backslash) followed by cell address containing header or footer text.

(continued)

PRINTING (continued)

8. **ENTER** .... ↵
9. Press **ESC** .... Esc
10. Press **R** (Range) .... R
11. Highlight range to be printed.
12. **ENTER** .... ↵
13. Press **A** (Align) .... A
14. Press **G** (Go) .... G
15. Press **Q** (Quit) .... Q

NOTE: - *To print the date automatically:*
  - *Type an @ symbol as part of header/footer text.*
- *To print a page number automatically:*
  - *Type a # symbol as part of header/footer text.*

EXAMPLES:

Entry: @ ¦ JANUARY SALES ¦¦ Page#
Resulting Header:

6/30/91	JANUARY SALES	Page 1

Entry: JANUARY SALES ¦¦ Page#
Resulting Header:

JANUARY SALES	Page 1

(continued)

An Encoded File

*NOTE: This feature creates a file that can be printed through the DOS **copy** command to a printer. See your DOS manual for more information on printing an encoded file.*

1. Place cursor on first cell to be printed.
2. Press / (Menu) .... [/]
3. Press **P** (Printer).. [P]
4. Press **E** (Encoded)... [E]
5. Type name of encoded file ....**Option**
6. **ENTER** .... [↵]
7. Press **R** (Range)... [R]
8. Press **.** (period) to lock in the range.......................... [.]
9. Highlight range to be printed.
10. **ENTER** .... [↵]
11. Select any formatting options.
12. Press **A** (Align) .... [A]
13. Press **G** (Go).. [G]
14. Press **Q** (Quit).. [Q]

(continued)

Controlling the Printer

1. Press / (Menu) .... /
2. Press **P** (Printer).. P
3. Select an option for controlling the printer:

   S (Suspend) Suspends printing.............. S

   R (Resume) Resumes printing .... R

   C (Cancel) Cancels all print jobs.......... C

PROTECTING THE WORKSHEET

NOTE: Will protect worksheet from changes.

1. Press **/** (Menu) .... /
2. Press **W** (Worksheet) .... W
3. Press **G** (Global) .... G
4. Press **P** (Protection) .... P
5. Press **E** (Enable) .... E

   -OR- OR

   Press **D** (Disable) .... D

QUERYING A DATABASE/FINDING EXTRACTING RECORDS

NOTE: The "input", "criteria" and "output" ranges must be created before Data Query/FIND, EXTRACT, UNIQUE, or DELETE functions can be used.

Creating the Input Range

(The range containing database records to be queried.)

1. Press / (Menu) .... /
2. Press **D** (Data) .... D
3. Press **Q** (Query) .... Q
4. Press **I** (Input) I
5. Type or highlight "input" range which can be from multiple worksheets.

   NOTE: The first row of the range must include the field names.

6. **ENTER** .... ↵
7. Press **ESC** three times to return to READY mode.................. Esc Esc Esc

(continued)

QUERYING A DATABASE/FINDING EXTRACTING RECORDS (continued)

Creating the Criteria Range

8. • Place cursor in a cell in an available area of the worksheet.
   • Type the exact field names used in the input range.

   -OR-

   • Copy field names from input range to an available area of the worksheet.

9. Place cursor in a cell below field to be searched (in criteria range).

10. Type search criteria. (Data to be searched FOR.)

11. **ENTER** .... ↵

    NOTE: Repeat steps 9-11 for each field to be searched.

12. Press / (Menu) .... /

13. Press **D** (Data) .... D

14. Press **Q** (Query) .... Q

15. Press **C** (Criteria) C

16. Type or highlight "output" range.

    NOTE: The first row of the range must include the field names.

17. **ENTER** .... ↵

18. Press **ESC** three times to return to READY mode.............. Esc Esc Esc

(continued)

QUERYING A DATABASE/FINDING EXTRACTING RECORDS (continued)

Creating the Output Range

1. • Place cursor in a cell in an available area of the worksheet.
   • Type the exact field names used in the input range.

   -OR-

   • Copy field names from input range to an available area of the worksheet.
2. Press / (Menu) .... [/]
3. Press **D** (Data) .... [D]
4. Press **Q** (Query) .... [Q]
5. Press **O** (Output) .... [O]
6. Type or highlight "output" range.

   NOTE: The first row of the range must include field names that match field names in input and criteria ranges. However, output range field names may be in any order.
7. **ENTER** .... [↵]

(continued)

QUERYING A DATABASE/FINDING EXTRACTING RECORDS (continued)

Extracting (Copying) Records In The Database to Output Range

8. • Press **E** (Extract) .... E
   to obtain records that meet the criteria and copy them to the output range.

   NOTE: If the output range does not contain enough room for the data, an error message will appear; it will then be necessary to create a larger output range.

   -OR- OR

   • Press U (Unique) to obtain **unique** records .... U
   (Duplicate records <u>will not</u> be copied to the output range.)

9. Press **Q** (Quit) .... Q
   to view output.

Finding Records In The Database

NOTE: Highlights records in input range that match specified criteria.

1. Press **/** (Menu) .... /
2. Press **D** (Data) .... D
3. Press **Q** (Query) .... Q
4. Press **F** (Find) .... F
   (The cursor highlights the first record that meets the criteria.)

(continued)

QUERYING A DATABASE/FINDING EXTRACTING RECORDS (continued)

5. Use cursor Up and Down arrow keys.............. ↑ ↓
   to highlight next record(s) that
   meet the criteria.

6. **ESC** four times to return
   to READY mode.................. Esc Esc Esc Esc

Deleting Records In the Database

1. Press **/** (Menu) .... /

2. Press **D** (Data)... D

3. Press **Q** (Query)... Q

4. Press **I** (Input) I

5. Highlight record(s) in input range to be deleted.

6. Press **D** (Delete) .... D

7. Press **D** (Delete) .... D

   -OR- OR

   Press **C** (Cancel)... C

(continued)

Connecting to an External Database

NOTE: This feature connects Lotus 1-2-3 to data in a database program, such as dBase III. The driver for the database must be installed.

1. Press **/** (menu) .... /
2. Press **D** (Data) .... D
3. Press **E** (External) .... E
4. Press **U** (Use) .... U
5. Highlight the database driver.
6. **ENTER** .... ↵
7. Type the name of the directory of the external database .... **Option**
8. **ENTER** .... ↵
9. Type or highlight the name of the external table.
10. **ENTER** .... ↵
11. **ENTER** .... ↵
    to accept the database as the default range name.
12. Press **Q** (Quit) .... Q

(continued)

QUERYING A DATABASE/FINDING EXTRACTING RECORDS (continued)

Copying Data from an External Database

NOTE: This feature extracts data from a connected database.

1. Press / (menu) .... /
2. Press **D** (Data).................... D
3. Press **E** (External).................... E
4. Press **L** (List).................... L
5. Press **F** (Fields) .... F
6. Highlight the range name of the external data.
7. **ENTER** .... ↵
8. Place cursor in the location for the data table.
9. **ENTER** .... ↵
10. Press **Q** (Quit).................... Q
11. Place cursor in the first cell of the external table.
12. Press / (menu) .... /
13. Press **R** (Range).................... R
14. Press **T** (Transpose).................... T
15. Highlight down to the last field name.
16. **ENTER** .... ↵

(continued)

QUERYING A DATABASE/FINDING EXTRACTING RECORDS (continued)

17. **ENTER** .... ↵
    to transpose the range across the top line of the data.
18. Place cursor in the bottom right corner of the table.
19. Press / (menu) .... /
20. Press **R** (Range) .... R
21. Press **E** (Erase) .... E
22. Highlight the cell below the top left corner of the table.
23. **ENTER** .... ↵
24. Place cursor in the first cell of the field name.
25. Press / (menu) .... /
26. Press **C** (Copy) C
27. Highlight the field names.
28. **ENTER** .... ↵
29. Move cursor to the first cell for the criteria which has a blank row below.
30. **ENTER** .... ↵
31. Place cursor in the first cell of the field name that was part of the table.
32. Press / (menu) .... /

(continued)

QUERYING A DATABASE/FINDING EXTRACTING RECORDS (continued)

33. Press **C** (Copy) C
34. Highlight the field names.
35. **ENTER** .... ↵
36. Move cursor to the first cell of the output.
37. **ENTER** .... ↵
38. Press **/** (menu) .... /
39. Press **D** (Data) .... D
40. Press **Q** (Query) .... Q
41. Press **I** (Input) I
42. Press **F3** (Name) F3
43. Highlight range name of the external file.
44. **ENTER** .... ↵
45. Press **C** (Criteria) C
46. Highlight fields of the criteria range and the blank row below it.
47. **ENTER** .... ↵
48. Press **O** (Output) .... O
49. Highlight fields of the output range.
50. **ENTER** .... ↵
51. Press **E** (Extract) .... E
52. Press **Q** (Quit) .... Q

QUITTING

1. Press / (Menu) .... /
2. Press **Q** (Quit).. Q
3. Type **Y** to quit.. Y
   if worksheet is already saved.

   -OR- OR

   - Type **Y** to quit.................................. Y
   - Type **Y** to confirm.............................. Y
     if worksheet is not saved.

   -OR- OR

   - Type **N** (to return to worksheet) .... N

OPTION:

4. Type **E** (Exit) .... E

RETRIEVING A FILE

NOTE: The retrieved worksheet will replace the worksheet currently on the screen.

1. Type / (Menu) .... /
2. Type **F** (File) .... F
3. Type **R** (Retrieve) .... R
4. Type filename to be retrieved.

   -OR-

   Highlight filename to be retrieved using cursor arrow keys.
5. **ENTER** .... ↵

Retrieving Files in a Different Drive/Directory

1. Follow steps 1-3 above.
2. Press **ESC** twice .... Esc Esc
3. Type new drive and/or directory.
4. **ENTER** .... ↵
5. Highlight filename to be retrieved using cursor arrow keys.
6. **ENTER** .... ↵

SAVING A FILE

NOTE: When a file is saved, Lotus 1-2-3 assigns a .WK3 extension to the filename unless a different extension is specified.

Saving a New Worksheet

1. Press **/** (Menu) .... /
2. Press **F** (File) .... F
3. Press **S** (Save)... S
4. Type a filename
   to save into the current directory.

   -OR-

   To save into a different directory:

   - Press **ESC** three times .... Esc Esc Esc
   - Type a new drive and / or directory.
   - Type a filename.
5. **ENTER** ....

Re-Saving/Overwriting a Worksheet

1. Press **/** (Menu) .... /
2. Press **F** (File) .... F
3. Press **S** (Save)... S

(continued)

SAVING A FILE (continued)

4. **ENTER** .... ↵

- Type name of file if it is not displayed.

5. Press **R** (Replace) .... R
   to replace an existing file with the new file.

   -OR- OR

   Press **B** (Backup)... B
   to create a backup file with the extension .BAK while maintaining the existing file with the extension .WK3.

   -OR- OR

   Press **C** (Cancel)... C
   to cancel the operation.

Saving a Portion of Current Worksheet as a New File

1. Press **/** (Menu) .... /
2. Press **F** (File) .... F
3. Press **X** (Xtract)... X
4. Select a saving option:

   F To save formulas and cell contents from current worksheet to new worksheet.......................... F

   V To save results of formulas and labels as a new worksheet............................... V

(continued)

SAVING A FILE (continued)

5. Type a new filename.
6. Highlight range of worksheet to be saved as a separate file.
7. **ENTER** .... ↵

Saving a File with a Password

NOTE: Password names are case sensitive.

1. Press **/** (Menu) .... /
2. Press **F** (File) .... F
3. Press **S** (Save) .... S
4. Type a filename.
5. Press **SPACEBAR** once .... Space
6. Press **P** (Password) .... P
7. **ENTER** .... ↵
8. Type a password.
9. **ENTER** .... ↵
10. Type password again (at 'Verify' prompt).
11. **ENTER** .... ↵

    If Updating the File:

12. Press **R** (Replace) .... R

(continued)

SAVING A FILE (continued)

Changing a Password

1. Press / (Menu) .... /
2. Press **F** (File) .... F
3. Press **S** (Save) .... S
4. Press **BACKSPACE** once .... Backspace
   to clear 'Password Protected' prompt.
5. Follow steps 4-12 beginning on previous page.

Deleting a Password

1. Type / (Menu) .... /
2. Type **F** (File) .... F
3. Type **S** (Save) .... S
4. Press **BACKSPACE** once .... Backspace
   to clear 'Password Protected' prompt.
5. **ENTER** .... ↵
6. Type **R** (Replace) .... R
   to update file without a password.

SEARCHING A RANGE
for Character Strings

NOTE: Searches for character strings in labels and / or formulas within a specified range.

1. Press / (Menu) .... [/]
2. Press **R** (Range) .... [R]
3. Press **S** (Search) .... [S]
4. Highlight the range to be searched.
5. **ENTER** .... [↵]
6. Type the string to be searched FOR.
7. **ENTER** .... [↵]
8. Select a desired option:

   F Searches for formulas .... [F]

   L Searches for labels .... [L]

   B Searches for both labels and formulas ..... [B]
9. Press **F** (Find) .... [F]
   to highlight first occurrence of search string.
10. Press **N** (Next) .... [N]
    to search for next occurrence.

    -OR- OR

    Press **Q** (Quit) .... [Q]
    to cancel operation.

(continued)

SEARCHING A RANGE (continued)

Replacing a Character String

1. Press / (Menu) .... [/]
2. Press **R** (Range).. [R]
3. Press **S** (Search) .... [S]
4. Highlight the range to be searched.
5. **ENTER** .... [↵]
6. Type the string to be searched for.
7. **ENTER** .... [↵]
8. Select a desired option:

   F Searches for formulas.......................... [F]

   L Searches for labels.............................. [L]

   B Searches for both labels and formulas.. [B]

9. Press **R** (Replace) .... [R]
10. Type the replacement string.
11. **ENTER** .... [↵]

(continued)

SEARCHING A RANGE (continued)

12. Select a desired option when first occurrence is highlighted:

    R Replaces current string with replacement string .... R

    A Replaces ALL remaining occurrences with replacement string .... A

    N Finds the next occurrence................. N

    Q Stops search .... Q

13. **ENTER** .... ↵
    to return to READY mode.

SETTING DEFAULTS

NOTE: • *Settings apply globally during the current work session. If current settings are desired for future work sessions, they may be saved through /**W**orksheet **G**lobal **D**efault **U**pdate in a file called 123.CNF.*
• *The current status of settings should be reviewed before changes are made.*

Viewing Default Setting Status

1. Press / (Menu) .... /
2. Press **W** (Worksheet) .... W
3. Press **G** (Global) .... G
4. Press **D** (Default) .... D
5. Press **S** (Status) .... S

Changing Default Settings

1. Press / (Menu) .... /
2. Press **W** (Worksheet) .... W
3. Press **G** (Global) .... G
4. Press **D** (Default) .... D

(continued)

SETTING DEFAULTS (continued)

5. Select a default setting option:

A (Autoexec).. A
Directs Lotus 1-2-3 whether or not to run an autoexec macro.

- Press **Y** (Yes). ..... Y to automatically execute a macro.

-OR-

- Press **N** (No). ...... N not to automatically execute a macro.

D (Directory).. D
Sets drive and directory names.

- Type desired directory ....**Option**
- **ENTER**................ 

G (Graph).. G
Sets graph ranges and file formats.

- Press **C** (Columnwise) .....  to create automatic graph data ranges by columns.

-OR-

- Press **R** (Rows) .. R to create automatic graph data ranges by rows.

(continued)

SETTING DEFAULTS (continued)

-OR-

- Press **M** (Metafile)............ M to save graphs as CGM files.

-OR-

- Press **P** (PIC) ...... P to save graphs as PIC files.

P (Printer).. 

- Press **A**............... A to control printer signal at each line of output.
- Press **Y** (Yes). ..... Y not to send line feeds.

-OR- OR

- Press **N** (No)........ N to send line feeds.

-OR-

- Press **B**............... B to set bottom page default.
- Type number of desired lines for bottom margin..**Option**
- **ENTER** .... ↵

(continued)

SETTING DEFAULTS (continued)

-OR-

- Press **I**.................. [I] to identify interface or port.
- Type desired option.

-OR-

- Press **L**................ [L] to set left margin default.
- Type desired left margin ....**Option**
- **ENTER**................. [↵]

-OR-

- Press **N**............... [N] to name additional printer(s) being used.
- Highlight printer to be used.

-OR-

- Press **P**................ [P] to set page length.
- Type number of desired page length......**Option**
- **ENTER**................. [↵]

(continued)

SETTING DEFAULTS (continued)

-OR-

- Press **R** .... R
  to set right
  margin default.
- Type desired
  right margin.....**Option**
- **ENTER** .... ↵

-OR-

- Press **S**............... S
  to indicate printer
  setup string.
- Type desired
  setup string......**Option**
- **ENTER** .... ↵

-OR-

- Press **T**............... T
  to set top margin.
- Type number
  of desired lines
  for top margin...**Option**
- **ENTER** .... ↵

-OR-

- Press **W** .... W
  to pause after
  each printed page.
- Press **Y** (Yes) ...... Y
  to pause after
  each page.

(continued)

SETTING DEFAULTS (continued)

-OR-

- Press **N** (No) .... [N] not to pause after each page.

O (Other)... [O]
Sets clock formats, help access method, beep, International settings and undo feature.

Select an "Other" option:

A (Add-In) .... [A]

- Press **S**................ [S] to set an auto-attach add-in.
- Type desired number (1-8) of auto-attach add-in....**Option**
- Type or highlight file name of add-in.
- **ENTER** .... [↵]

-OR-

- Press **C**................ [C] to detach add-in.

(continued)

SETTING DEFAULTS (continued)

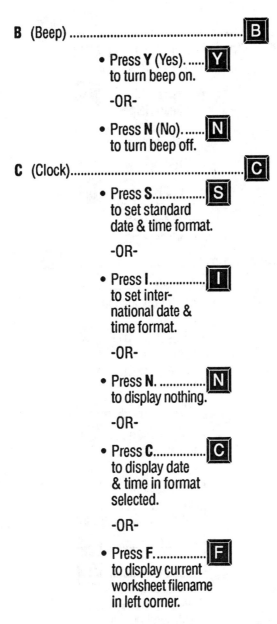

B (Beep) .... B

- Press **Y** (Yes). ..... Y
  to turn beep on.

  -OR-

- Press **N** (No). ...... N
  to turn beep off.

C (Clock)... C

- Press **S**............... S
  to set standard
  date & time format.

  -OR-

- Press **I**................ I
  to set inter-
  national date &
  time format.

  -OR-

- Press **N**. .... N
  to display nothing.

  -OR-

- Press **C**............... C
  to display date
  & time in format
  selected.

  -OR-

- Press **F**............... F
  to display current
  worksheet filename
  in left corner.

(continued)

SETTING DEFAULTS (continued)

H (Help) .... H

NOTE: The help options have no effect in release 3.1 of Lotus 1-2-3.

- Press **I** I
  to keep Help open during work session.

  -OR-

- Press **R** .... R
  to open and close Help for each work session.

I (International) I

- Press **P** .... P
  to set punctuation symbols.
- Press **A-F** ... A - F
  to select desired punctuation format.

  -OR-

- Press **C** C
  to set currency symbols.
- Type desired currency symbol .... **Option**
- **ENTER** .... ↵
- Press **P** .... P
  to precede currency value with symbol.

(continued)

SETTING DEFAULTS (continued)

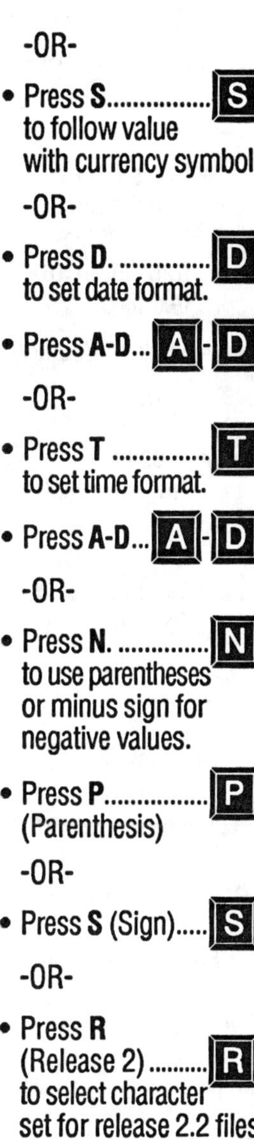

-OR-

- Press **S**................ S
  to follow value
  with currency symbol.

-OR-

- Press **D**. .... D
  to set date format.
- Press **A-D**... A - D

-OR-

- Press **T** .... T
  to set time format.
- Press **A-D**... A - D

-OR-

- Press **N**. .... N
  to use parentheses
  or minus sign for
  negative values.
- Press **P**................ P
  (Parenthesis)

-OR-

- Press **S** (Sign)..... S

-OR-

- Press **R**
  (Release 2) .... R
  to select character
  set for release 2.2 files.
- Press **L** (LICS) L

(continued)

SETTING DEFAULTS (continued)

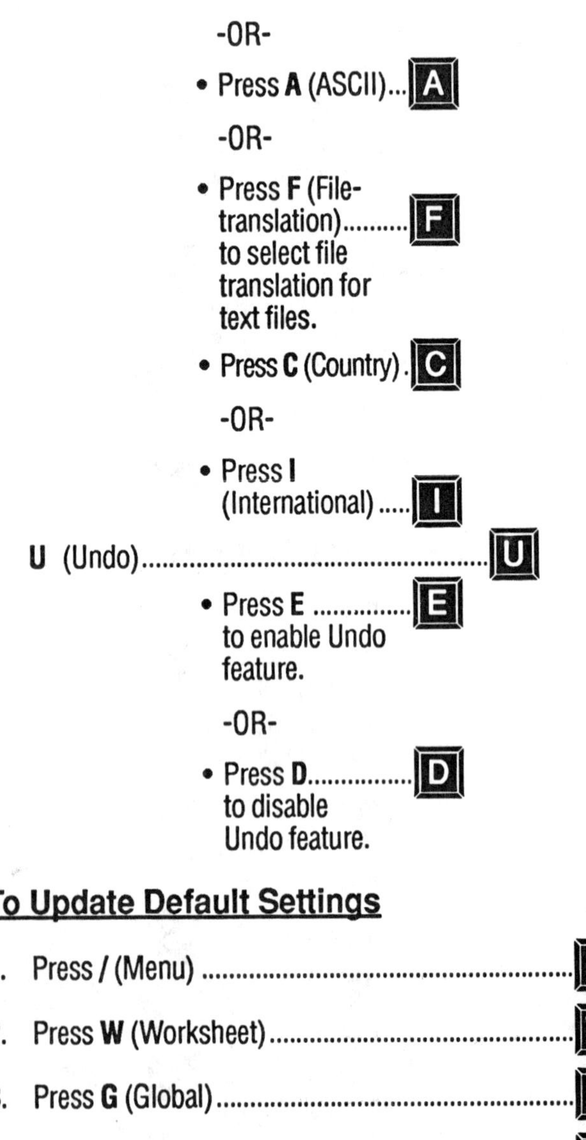

-OR-

- Press **A** (ASCII)... A

-OR-

- Press **F** (File-translation).......... F to select file translation for text files.
- Press **C** (Country) . C

-OR-

- Press **I** (International) I

U (Undo)... U

- Press **E** .... E to enable Undo feature.

-OR-

- Press **D**............... D to disable Undo feature.

To Update Default Settings

1. Press / (Menu) .... /
2. Press **W** (Worksheet)....................................... W
3. Press **G** (Global).. G
4. Press **D** (Default)... D
5. Press **U** (Update)... U

USING SOLVER

*NOTE: This **add-in** feature allows the operator to perform complex "what-if" problems.*

Attaching Solver Add-In/Selecting

1. Press **Alt + F10** (Addin) .... Alt + F10
2. Press **L** (Load) L
3. Highlight **SOLVER.PLC.**
4. **ENTER** .... ↵
5. **ENTER** .... ↵
   to not assign add-in to a key.
6. Press **I** (Invoke) I
7. Highlight **SOLVER.**
8. **ENTER** .... ↵

Defining the Cells

1. Press **D** (Define) .... D
2. Select the cell to be defined:

   A (Adjustable) Identifies cells containing data that will be changed in the worksheet .... A

   - Highlight or type address of adjustable cell(s).
   - **ENTER** .... ↵

(continued)

USING SOLVER (continued)

C (Constraints) Identifies cells containing logical formulas each Solver answer must satisfy C

- Highlight or type address of constraint cell(s).
- **ENTER** .... ↵

O (Optimal) Identifies optimal cells that Solver answer must find highest or lowest value .... O

-Select the kind of optimal cell:

-**X**-Maximize X

- Highlight or type address of optimal cell.
- **ENTER** .... ↵

-OR-

-**N**-Minimize .... N

- Highlight or type address of optimal cell.
- **ENTER** .... ↵

-OR-

-Reset .... R

Q (Quit) Quits Define Cell Menu .... Q

Answering the Problem

1. Press **A** (Answer) .... A

(continued)

USING SOLVER (continued)

2. Select the answer option:

F (First)	Shows first attempt or answer to problem	F
L (Last)	Shows last attempt or answer to problem	L
N (Next)	Shows next attempt or answer to problem	N

NOTE: If the last answer is displayed, the first one will be shown.

O (Optimal)	Shows optimal answer to problem if available	O
P (Previous)	Shows previous attempt or answer to problem	P

NOTE: If the first answer is displayed, the last one will be shown.

R (Reset)	Returns adjustable cells to values before Solver found answers	R
Q (Quit)	Quits Answer Menu	Q

Solving the Problem

NOTE: If selecting "Guesses", first use the "Answers" command to show the attempt which prompts with "Guesses required".

1. Press **S** (Solve) S

(continued)

USING SOLVER (continued)

2. Select the option for solving the problem:

   C (Continue) Finds the number of answers specified by the Options Number-Answers C

   G (Guesses) Enters guesses for adjustable cells and then attempts to solve using the values .... G

   -Select the Guesses option:

   -**G**uess .... G

   - Type a guess value for adjustable cell.
   - **ENTER** .... ↵

   -**N**ext .... N

   -OR-

   -**S**olve .... S

   -**Q**uit .... Q

   P (Problem) Solves the problem .... P

Producing Solver Reports

1. Press **R** (Report) .... R
2. Select the report option:

   A (Answer) Creates a worksheet in a new file, named ANSWER01.WK3, containing the optimal answer (if available), the optimal cells, adjustable cells, and supporting formula cells. .... A

(continued)

USING SOLVER (continued)

C (Cells) Reports adjustable, constraint and optimal cells........ C

-Select the output format:

-**C**ell........ C
to create a window on the cells.

-Press **N** (Next)........ N

-OR-

-Press **Q** (Quit)........ Q

-**T**able........ T
to create a worksheet in a new file, named CELLS001.WK3, on the cells containing the optimal cells, adjustable cells, and constraint cells.

D (Differences) Compares two attempts or answers and reports problem cells that differ by specified value........ D

-Select the output format:

-**C**ell........ C
to create a window on cell differences containing answers, differences, and percentages for differences.

-OR-

-**T**able........ T
to create a worksheet in a new file, named DIFFS001.WK3, containing the range names, differences, percentages for differences, original numbers, and minimum differences.

- Type the value for the answer.

(continued)

USING SOLVER (continued)

- **ENTER** .... [↵]
- Type the value for the other answer.
- **ENTER** .... [↵]
- Type the amount of difference between answers for which Solver is to repeat.
- **ENTER** .... [↵]

-If cell was selected, then:

-Press **N** (Next) .... [N]

-OR-

-Press **Q** (Quit) .... [Q]

H (How) Creates a worksheet in a new file, called HOW0001.WK3, containing steps for solving problem .... [H]

I (Inconsistent) Reports constraint cells that were false and reports revised logical formulas .... [I]

NOTE: Inconsistent Reports are only available when showing an attempt in the worksheet.

-Select the output format:

-**C**ell .... [C]
to create a window that contains constraint cells.

-OR-

(continued)

USING SOLVER (continued)

-Table .... T
to create a worksheet in a new file, named INCONS01.WK3, containing the range names and constraint cells.

U (Unused) Reports unused constraints and adjustments needed to make them affect the answer......... U

-Select the output format:

-**C**ell C
to create a window that contains constraint cells and adjustments.

-OR-

-Table .... T
to create a worksheet in a new file, named UNUSED01.WK3, containing the range name, adjustment, and constraint cells.

-If cell was selected, then:

-Press **N** (Next) .... N

-OR-

-Press **Q** (Quit)...................................... Q

W (What-If) Reports value for an adjustable cell that meets constraints .... W

-Select the output format:

-**C**ell C
to create a window containing the highest and lowest values of the adjustable cells that meet constraints.

(continued)

USING SOLVER (continued)

-OR-

-Table .... T
to create a worksheet in a new file, named LIMITS01.WK3, containing a range name (if it exists) and the highest and lowest values of the adjustable cells that meet constraints.

-If cell was selected, then:

-Press **N** (Next) .... N

-OR-

-Press **Q** (Quit) .... Q

Options for Solver Reports

NOTE: The default number of answers is 10.

1. Press **O** (Option) .... O
2. Press **N** (Number-Answers) .... N
3. Type the number of answers for Solver to calculate.
4. **ENTER** .... ↵

SORTING DATA

NOTE: Sorting may be accomplished on one or two columns (fields) in ascending or descending order.

1. Press / (Menu) .... /
2. Press **D** (Data) .... D
3. Press **S** (Sort) .... S
4. Press **D** (Data-Range) .... D
5. Type or highlight* data range to be sorted.

   **NOTE:* Labels at the top of the database SHOULD NOT be included when highlighting since they will be sorted along with the data.*

6. **ENTER** .... ↵
7. Press **P** (Primary-Key) .... P
8. Place cursor in column to be primary sorted.
9. **ENTER** .... ↵
10. Type **A** (Ascending) .... A

    -OR- OR

    Type **D** (Descending) .... D
11. **ENTER** .... ↵

(continued)

SORTING DATA (continued)

OPTIONAL
To Sort on Secondary Field:

- Press **S** (Secondary Key) .... [S]
- Place cursor in column to be secondary sorted.
- **ENTER** .... [↵]
- Type **A** (Ascending) .... [A]

  -OR- OR

- Type **D** (Descending) .... [D]
- **ENTER** .... [↵]

12. Press **G** (Go) .... [G]

OPTIONAL
To Sort on Additional Fields

- Press **E** (Extra Key) .... [E]
- Type number of extra key .... **Option**

NOTE: Up to 255 extra sort keys can be added, but they must be consecutive, beginning with number 1.

- **ENTER** .... [↵]
- Place cursor in column of extra sort key.

(continued)

SORTING DATA (continued)

- **ENTER** .... ↵
- Type **A** (Ascending) .... A

  -OR- OR

- Type **D** (Descending) .... D
- **ENTER** .... ↵
- Repeat above steps for additional sort keys.

TRANSPOSING DATA

NOTE: Transposes data from horizontal to vertical arrangement and vice versa. Formulas are replaced by values.

1. Press / (Menu) .... /
2. Press **R** (Range) .... R
3. Press **T** (Trans) .... T
4. Highlight range to be transposed.
5. **ENTER** .... ↵
6. Place cursor on first available cell to receive transposed data.
7. **ENTER** .... ↵

UNDO (Previous Command)

NOTE: • Lotus 1-2-3 must be in READY mode, and UNDO must be enabled.
• UNDO cannot be used a second time to restore the changes that were just made.

1. Press **Alt + F4** (Undo).................................. Alt + F4

2. Press **Y** (Yes).. Y
   to undo command.

   -OR- OR

   Press **N** (No).. N
   to not undo command.

UPGRADING LOTUS 1-2-3 3.0 FILES TO 3.1 AND 3.1+

1. Retrieve 3.0 file to be upgraded.
2. Press / (Menu) .... /
3. Press **W** (Worksheet) .... W
4. Press **S** (Status) .... S
5. Note order of recalculation: Natural, Rowwise, or Columnwise.
6. **ENTER** .... ↵
7. Press / (Menu) .... /
8. Press **W** (Worksheet) .... W
9. Press **G** (Global) .... G
10. Press **R** (Recalc) .... R
11. Select a recalculation not currently selected:

    R (Rowwise) .... R

    N (Natural) .... N

    C (Columnwise) C
12. Press **F9** (Calc) F9
13. Press / (Menu) .... /
14. Press **W** (Worksheet) .... W

(continued)

UPGRADING LOTUS 1-2-3 (continued)

15. Press **G** (Global) .... [G]

16. Press **R** (Recalc) .... [R]

17. Select the original recalculation method:

    R (Rowwise) .... [R]

    N (Natural) .... [N]

    C (Columnwise) .... [C]

18. Press **F9** (Calc) .... [F9]

19. Press / (Menu) .... [/]

20. Press **F** (File) .... [F]

21. Press **S** (Save) .... [S]

22. **ENTER** .... [↵]

23. Press **R** (Replace) .... [R]

USING VIEWER

NOTE: This add-in feature allows the operator to view the contents of a worksheet, text, and database file on disk or on a network. The operator can browse through, open, retrieve, and/or link files.

1. Press **Alt + F10** (Addin) .... Alt + F10
2. Press **L** (Load) L
3. Highlight **VIEWER.PLC**.
4. **ENTER** .... ↵
5. **ENTER** .... ↵
   to not assign add-in to a key.
6. Press **I** (Invoke) I
7. Highlight **VIEWER**.
8. **ENTER** .... ↵
9. Select a viewer option:

   R (Retrieve) .... R

   L (Link) L

   O (Open) .... O

   B (Browse) .... B
10. Follow steps 5 to end of procedures outlined on following pages to "**Retrieve**", "**Open**", "**Link**", or "**Browse**".

(continued)

USING VIEWER (continued)

Browsing a File Using View

1. Press **Alt + F10** (Addin) .... Alt + F10
2. Press **I** (Invoke) I
3. Highlight **VIEWER.**
4. **ENTER** .... ↵
5. Press **B** (Browse) .... B
6. Press **Up/Down arrow** keys to highlight file to view .... ↑, ↓

   NOTE: Files will appear on the right of screen.

7. Press **ESC** .... Esc
   to exit view.
8. Press **ESC** .... Esc
   to exit menu.

Retrieving a File

1. Press **Alt + F10** (Addin) .... Alt + F10
2. Press **I** (Invoke) I
3. Highlight **VIEWER.**
4. **ENTER** .... ↵

(continued)

USING VIEWER (continued)

5. Press **R** (Retrieve) .... R

- Save current worksheet file if necessary.

6. Press **Up/Down arrow** keys to highlight file to retrieve .... ↑, ↓

7. **ENTER** .... ↵

Opening a File

1. Press **Alt + F10** (Addin) .... Alt + F10

2. Press **I** (Invoke) I

3. Highlight **VIEWER.**

4. **ENTER** .... ↵

5. Press **O** (Open) .... O

6. Press **B** (Before) .... B

   -OR- OR

   Press **A** (After) .... A

7. Press **Up/Down arrow** keys to highlight file to open .... ↑, ↓

8. **ENTER** .... ↵

- Enter password if necessary.

(continued)

USING VIEWER (continued)

Linking a File

1. Place cursor in cell that will be linked to other worksheet.
2. Press **Alt + F10** (Addin) .... Alt + F10
3. Press **I** (Invoke) I
4. Highlight **VIEWER.**
5. **ENTER** .... ↵
6. Press **L** (Link) L
7. Press **Up/Down arrow** keys to highlight file to link .... ↑, ↓
8. Press **Right Arrow** key to specify cell or range of cells to link .... →
9. Press **.** (Period) ....
   to lock in the range.
10. Highlight range.
11. **ENTER** .... ↵

NOTE: Cell will display formula preceeded by linked file, e.g. ***+<<c:\123R3\JOEFUSCO.WK3>>A:B1.***

WINDOWS

1. Place cursor one ROW below or one COLUMN to the right of where split is to occur.
2. Press / (Menu) .... /
3. Press **W** (Worksheet) .... W
4. Press **W** (Window) .... W
5. Select a screen split option:

   H (Horizontal) .... H

   V (Vertical) V

To Select A Scrolling Option:

6. Repeat steps 2-4 above.
7. Press **S** (Sync) .... S
   to synchronize scrolling.

   -OR- OR

   Press **U** (Unsync) .... U
   to unsynchronize scrolling.

   *NOTE: Press **F6** to move from one window to another.*

WORKSHEET

Status

NOTE: Will display the current global worksheet settings status.

1. Press / (Menu) .... /
2. Press **W** (Worksheet) .... W
3. Press **S** (Status) .... S
4. Press any key to return to worksheet.

Perspective

NOTE: This feature displays three consecutive worksheets in "3D" perspective.

1. Press / (Menu) .... /
2. Press **W** (Worksheet) .... W
3. Press **W** (Window) .... W
4. Press **P** (Perspective) .... P

*NOTE: Press **F6** to move between the worksheets.*

(continued)

Clearing Window

1. Press / (Menu) .... /
2. Press **W** (Worksheet) .... W
3. Press **W** (Window) .... W
4. Press **C** (Clear) C

Map View

NOTE: This feature displays "#" in cells with numbers, "+" in annotated or formula cells, and ' " ' in cells with labels.

1. Press / (Menu) .... /
2. Press **W** (Worksheet) .... W
3. Press **W** (Window) .... W
4. Press **M** (Map View) .... M
5. Press **E** (Enable) .... E
6. Press **ESC** (Escape) .... Esc

USING WYSIWYG (What You See Is What You Get)

*NOTE: This **add-in** feature allows the operator to change the appearance of data. However, printers must be able to support this feature and monitors must be able to display this feature. Otherwise, Lotus 1-2-3 will substitute the closest available font your printer will support or display the closest available color your monitor will show.*

Attaching WYSIWYG Add-In

NOTE: When WYSIWYG is activated, the word "WYSIWYG" will display at the top right of the screen.

1. Press **Alt + F10** (Addin) .... Alt + F10
2. Press **L** (Load) L
3. Highlight **WYSIWYG.PLC.**
4. **ENTER** .... ↵
5. **ENTER** .... ↵
   to not assign add-in to a key.
6. Press **I** (Invoke) I
7. **ENTER** .... ↵

(continued)

USING WYSIWYG (continued)

NOTE: The word WYSIWYG should be displayed at the top right of the screen and the Wysiwyg menu should appear. To leave the Wysiwyg menu and activate the regular menu, press ESC and / (slash). To leave the regular menu and return to the Wysiwyg menu, press ESC and : (colon).

Changing Fonts

NOTE:
- *A typeface is the design of a character. Lotus 1-2-3 provides four typefaces: Swiss, Dutch, Courier and Xsymbol.*
- *A point size is a unit of measure of a character.*
- *A font is a particular typeface in a particular point size. Up to eight fonts may be used in a worksheet.*

Lotus 1-2-3 provides the following fontsets: Swiss in 12, 14 and 24 point; Dutch in 6, 8, 10 and 12 point; and Xsymbol in 12 point.

1. Press : (Colon) .... [:]
   if you are not in the WYSIWYG menu.

2. Press **F** (Format) .... [F]

3. Press **F** (Font) .... [F]

4. Select a desired fontset:

   1 (Swiss 12 point) .... [1]

(continued)

USING WYSIWYG (continued)

2 (Swiss 14 point) .... [2]

3 (Swiss 24 point) .... [3]

4 (Dutch 6 point) .... [4]

5 (Dutch 8 point) .... [5]

6 (Dutch 10 point) .... [6]

7 (Dutch 12 point) .... [7]

8 (Xsymbol 12 point) .... [8]

5. Type range to receive fontset change.

6. **ENTER** .... [↵]

Changing Typestyles/Shading/Color

NOTE: • *A typestyle is the treatment of characters (mainly for emphasis) such as bold, italic, or underline. Ranges may also be shaded or colored (for color monitors and color printers).*
• *If already working in the :Format submenu, steps 1-2 need not be repeated.*

- Typestyles

1. Press : (Colon) .... [:]
   if you are not in the WYSIWYG menu.

2. Press **F** (Format) .... [F]

(continued)

USING WYSIWYG (continued)

3. Select one or more typestyle options:

   B (Bold) .... B

   -**S**et.. S

   -OR- OR

   -**C**lear.. C

   I (Italics) I

   -**S**et.. S

   -OR- OR

   -**C**lear.. C

   U (Underline) .... U

   -Select an underline option:

   -**S**ingle.. S

   -**D**ouble .... D

   -**W**ide .... W

   -**C**lear.. C

4. Type range to receive/remove typestyle change.

5. **ENTER**.. ↵

(continued)

USING WYSIWYG (continued)

- Color

NOTE: If already working in the :Format submenu, steps 1-2 need not be repeated.

1. Press : (Colon) .... :
   if you are not in the WYSIWYG menu.
2. Press **F** (Format).. F
3. Press **C** (Color) C
4. Select color change option:

   T (Text)
   Colors data in a range .... T

   -OR- OR

   B (Background)
   Selects background range color .... B

   Select a color:

   -**N**ormal .... N
   to return to default color.

   -**R**ed.. R

   -**G**reen.. G

   -**D**ark-Blue .... D

   -**C**yan C

   -**Y**ellow.. Y

(continued)

-**M**agenta .... [M]

- Type range to receive new color.
- **ENTER** .... [↵]

N (Negative)
Selects colors for negative range values.......... [N]

Select a color:

-**N**ormal.. [N]
to return to default color.

-**R**ed .... [R]

- Type range to receive new color.
- **ENTER** .... [↵]

R (Reverse) Reverses background and text colors in a range............ [R]

- Type range to receive reverse background.
- **ENTER** .... [↵]

-Shade

NOTE: If already working in the :Format submenu, steps 1-2 need not be repeated.

1. Press : (Colon) .... [:]
if you are not in the WYSIWYG menu.

(continued)

USING WYSIWYG (continued)

2. Press **F** (Format).. [F]
3. Press **S** (Shade).. [S]
4. Select a shading option:

   L (Light) .... [L]

   D (Dark).. [D]

   S (Solid) .... [S]

   C (Clear) .... [C]
5. Type range to be shaded.
6. **ENTER**.. [↵]

Using Lines

NOTE: If already working in the :Format submenu, steps 1-2 need not be repeated. This feature will add horizontal and vertical lines along the edges of cells in a range. Entire ranges or cells can be outlined using single, double or wide lines.

1. Press : (Colon) .... [:]
   if you are not in the WYSIWYG menu.
2. Press **F** (Format).. [F]
3. Press **L** (Lines).. [L]

(continued)

USING WYSIWYG (continued)

4. Select a line option:

O (Outline) Draws a single line outline around a range.......... O

- Type range to outline.
- **ENTER**.......... ↵

L (Left) Draws a single vertical line at left edge of each cell in a range.......... L

- Type range.
- **ENTER**.......... ↵

R (Right) Draws a single vertical line at right edge of each cell in a range.......... R

- Type range.
- **ENTER**.......... ↵

T (Top) Draws single horizontal line at top edge of each cell in a range.......... T

- Type range.
- **ENTER**.......... ↵

(continued)

USING WYSIWYG (continued)

B (Bottom) Draws single horizontal line at bottom edge of each cell in a range. .... B

- Type range.
- **ENTER** .... ↵

A (All) Draws single line outline around cells in a range......... A

- Type range.
- **ENTER** .... ↵

S (Shadow) Adds/removes a shadow from a range .... S

-**S**et .... S

- Type range.
- **ENTER** .... ↵

-**C**lear... C

  - Type range.
  - **ENTER** .... ↵

(continued)

To Set Double or Wide Lines:

1. Follow steps 1-3 on page 167 (Using Lines).
2. Select **D** (Double).. D

   -OR- OR

   Select **W** (Wide).. W
3. Follow step 4 (Line Options) on pages 168-169.

Resetting Changes/Quitting

NOTE: If already working in the :Format submenu, steps 1-2 need not be repeated.

1. Press : (Colon) .... :
   if you are not in the WYSIWYG menu.
2. Press **F** (Format).. F
3. Press **R** (Reset).. R
4. Type range to be reset.
5. **ENTER**.. ↵

(continued)

Changing Worksheet Display Options

NOTE: Changing display options affect the way a worksheet appears on the screen. It does not affect the printed worksheet or graphics.

- Cell Size

1. Press : (Colon) .... :
   if you are not in the WYSIWYG menu.

2. Press **D** (Display) .... D

3. Press **Z** (Zoom) .... Z

4. Select a cell size:

   T (Tiny) .... T

   S (Small) .... S

   N (Normal) .... N

   H (Huge) .... H

   M (Manual) .... M

   - Type scale factor ....**Option**
   - **ENTER** .... ↵

(continued)

- Colors

NOTE: If already working in the :Display submenu, steps 1-2 need not be repeated.

1. **Press : (Colon) .... :**
   if you are not in the WYSIWYG menu.
2. Press **D** (Display) .... D
3. Press **C** (Colors) C
4. Select item to change color:

   B (Background) .... B

   T (Text) .... T

   U (Unprot) .... U

   C (Cell pointer) C

   G (Grid) .... G

   F (Frame) .... F

   N (Neg) .... N

   L (Lines) L

   S (Shadow) .... S

(continued)

USING WYSIWYG (continued)

5. Select a color:

   Black.. B

   White.. W

   Green.. G

   Dark-Blue.. D

   Cyan... C

   Yellow... Y

   Magenta.. M

- Frame/Grid/Page Breaks/Cell Pointer/Intensity

NOTE: If already working in the :Display submenu, steps 1-2 need not be repeated.

1. Press : (Colon) .... :
   if you are not in the WYSIWYG menu.
2. Press **D** (Display).. D
3. Press **O** (Options).. O
4. Select an item to change:

   F (Frame)... F

(continued)

USING WYSIWYG (continued)

-**1** (1-2-3 frame)	Uses regular 1-2-3 frame	1
-**E** (Enhanced)	Displays enhanced WKS frame	E
-**R** (Relief)	Displays WKS frame in gray 3D	R
-**S** (Special)	Displays WKS frame in:	S
• **C**har	Characters per inch	C
• **I**nches	Inches	I
• **M**etric	Centimeters	M
• **P**oints	Points/picas	P
-**N** (None)	Displays no frame	N
G (Grid)	Turns worksheet grid on/off	G
-**N**o		N
-**Y**es		Y
P (Page-Breaks)	Displays or hides page-breaks in worksheet	P
-**Y**es		Y
-**N**o		N

(continued)

USING WYSIWYG (continued)

C (Cell-Pointer) Changes style of cell pointer .... [C]

-**S**olid .... [S]

-**O**utline .... [O]

I (Intensity) Changes screen brightness .... [I]

-**N**ormal .... [N]

-**H**igh .... [H]

- Rows

NOTE: If already working in the :Display submenu, steps 1-2 need not be repeated.

1. Press : (Colon) .... [:]
   if you are not in the WYSIWYG menu.
2. Press **D** (Display) .... [D]
3. Press **R** (Rows) .... [R]
4. Type number of rows to display.
5. **ENTER** .... [↵]

(continued)

- Restoring Defaults/Quitting

NOTE: If already working in the :Display submenu, steps 1-2 need not be repeated.

1. Press : (Colon) .... [:]
   if you are not in the WYSIWYG menu.
2. Press **D** (Display) .... [D]
3. Press **D** (Default) .... [D]
4. Press **R** (Restore) .... [R]

   -OR- OR

   Press **U** (Update) .... [U]

Adding / Editing /Viewing / Zooming Graphics

NOTE: Graphics may be added to a worksheet and edited to include text and other items, resized and reshaped.

- Adding a Graphic

1. **Press** : (Colon) .... [:]
   if you are not in the WYSIWYG menu.
2. Press **G** (Graph) .... [G]
3. Press **A** (Add) .... [A]

(continued)

USING WYSIWYG (continued)

4. Select type of graph to be added:

C (Current) Adds current graph to worksheet. C

-Type display range where graph appears.

-ENTER .... ↵

N (Named) Adds a named graph or graphic. .... N

-Type name of saved graph or graphic.

-ENTER .... ↵

P (PIC) Adds a graphic with a .PIC extension. .... P

-Highlight graphic file.

-ENTER .... ↵

-Type range to receive graphic.

-ENTER .... ↵

M (Metafile) Adds a graphic with a .CGM extension. .... M

-Highlight graphic file.

-ENTER .... ↵

-Type range to receive graphic.

-ENTER .... ↵

(continued)

USING WYSIWYG (continued)

B (Blank) Adds a placeholder for a graphic .... [B]

-Type range to receive placeholder.

-**ENTER** .... [↵]

- Editing a Graphic

1. Press : (Colon) .... [:]
   if you are not in the WYSIWYG menu.
2. Press **G** (Graph) .... [G]
3. Press **E** (Edit) .... [E]
4. Type range where graphic exists to edit.
5. Select an edit option:

   A (Add) Adds items to graphic. .... [A]

   Select item to add:

   -Text Adds text to graphic. .... [T]

   - Type text to be added.
   - **ENTER** .... [↵]
   - Move cursor to place text.
   - **ENTER** .... [↵]

   -Line Adds lines to graphic. .... [L]

(continued)

USING WYSIWYG (continued)

-**Polygon** Adds a polygon to graphic. .. [P]

-**Arrow** Adds an arrow to graphic..... [A]

- Move cursor to first point of line.
- **ENTER** .... [↵]
- Move cursor to next point of line.
- **ENTER** .... [↵]

-**Rectangle** Adds a rectangle to graphic .... [R]

- Move cursor to first corner.
- **ENTER** .... [↵]
- Move cursor to stretch the box.
- **ENTER** .... [↵]

-**Ellipse** Adds ellipse or circle to graphic. .... [E]

- Move cursor to first corner.
- **ENTER** .... [↵]
- Move cursor to stretch the box.
- **ENTER** .... [↵]

(continued)

USING WYSIWYG (continued)

-Freehand Allows for drawing freehand on graphic .... F

- Move cursor to first point.
- **ENTER** .... ↵
- Draw freehand.
- **ENTER** .... ↵

E (Edit) Changes text, fonts, width and style of lines, and adds and removes arrowheads in a graphic. This feature does not work on underlying graphics—only on items added to a graphic .... E

-**T**ext Edits text in a graphic .... T

-**C**entering Aligns text in a graphic C

- Highlight an alignment option:

  Left L

  Center C

  Right .... R

- Place cursor on text to be aligned.
- **ENTER** .... ↵

(continued)

USING WYSIWYG (continued)

-Font Changes fonts of text......... F

- Highlight desired point size.
- **ENTER** .... ↵
- Place cursor on text.
- **ENTER** .... ↵

-Line-Style Changes style of lines used in a graphic............... L

- Highlight a line-style option:

1-Solid.............................. 1

2-Dashed.......................... 2

3-Dotted 3

4-Long-Dashed................. 4

5-Chain-Dotted................. 5

6-Chained-Dashed............ 6

- **ENTER** .... ↵

-**W**idth Changes width of lines used in a graphic............... W

- Highlight a width option:

1-Very narrow 1

2-Narrow.......................... 2

(continued)

3-Medium........................ 3

4-Wide............................ 4

5-Very Wide...................... 5

- Place cursor on graphic to edit.
- **ENTER** .... ↵

-**A**rrowheads Changes arrowheads used in a graphic .... A

- Highlight arrowhead option:

Switch Changes direction arrowhead is pointing................ S

One Adds arrowhead to one end of line.................. O

Two Adds arrowheads to both ends of line.................. T

None Removes all arrowheads.......... N

- Place cursor on graphic to edit.
- **ENTER** .... ↵

Smoothing Smoothes corners of graphics.......................... S

(continued)

USING WYSIWYG (continued)

- Select a smooth option:

Medium Redraws graphic with maximal smoothing .... M

None Redraws smoothing.............. N

Tight Draws graph with outline that approximates original object.. T

- Place cursor on graphic to edit.
- **ENTER** .... ↵

T (Transform) .... T

Select a transform option:

-**S**ize Changes size of graphics... S

- Place cursor at top left corner of graphic.
- **ENTER** .... ↵
- Press Shift + Arrow keys to resize the box.
- **ENTER** .... ↵

-**R**otate Rotates graphics............. R

- Place cursor at top left corner of graphic.
- **ENTER** .... ↵
- Press arrow keys to rotate graphic.
- **ENTER** .... ↵

(continued)

USING WYSIWYG (continued)

-**Q**uarter-turn Rotates graphics at 90° increments.......................... Q

- **ENTER**.. ↵

-**X**-Flip Flips graphics horizontally.... X

- Place cursor at top left corner of graphic.
- **ENTER**.. ↵

-**Y**-Flip Flips graphics vertically....... Y

- Place cursor at top left corner of graphic.
- **ENTER**.. ↵

-**H**orizontal Skews graphic horizontally by width............ H

- Place cursor at top left corner of graphic.
- **ENTER**.. ↵
- Press arrow keys to rotate graphic.
- **ENTER**.. ↵

-**V**ertical Skews graphic vertically by length.............................. V

- Place cursor at top left corner of graphic.
- **ENTER**.. ↵
- Press arrow keys to slant the graphic.
- **ENTER**.. ↵

(continued)

USING WYSIWYG (continued)

-**C**lear — Clears all transformation changes.............................. C

- Place cursor at top edge of graphic.
- **ENTER** .... ↵

R (Rearrange) Deletes, restores, moves, copies locks and unlocks graphics.. R

-**D**elete — Deletes graphic .... D

- Place cursor at top left corner of graphic.
- **ENTER** .... ↵

-**R**estore — Restores graphic................. R

-**M**ove — Moves graphic .... M

- Press arrow keys to move graphic.
- **ENTER** .... ↵

-**C**opy — Copies graphic C

-**L**ock — Locks graphic from changes.. L

-**U**nlock — Unlocks graphic .... U

-**F**ront — Places graphic in front of others.............................. F

-**B**ack — Places graphic behind others .... B

(continued)

USING WYSIWYG (continued)

V (View) — Enlarges and reduces the size of the graphic editing window........ V

Select a view option:

-Full — Displays editing window full size........ F

-In — Displays a portion of editing window full screen........ I

- Place cursor in first corner.
- **ENTER**........ ↵
- Place cursor in last corner.
- **ENTER**........ ↵

-Pan — Moves editing window half-screen left, up, down........ P

-+ — Makes editing window appear larger........ +

— — Makes editing window appear smaller........ -

-Up — Moves editing window half-screen up........ U

-Down — Moves editing window half-screen down........ D

-Left — Moves editing window half-screen left........ L

-Right — Moves editing window half-screen right........ R

(continued)

USING WYSIWYG (continued)

-Viewing a Graphic

NOTE: For temporarily viewing a .PIC or CGM graphic file.

1. Press : (Colon) .... [:]
   if you are not in the WYSIWYG menu.
2. Press **G** (Graph) .... [G]
3. Press **V** (View) .... [V]
4. Press **P** (PIC) .... [P]

   -OR- OR

   Press **M** (Metafile) .... [M]
5. Highlight or type graph name.
6. **ENTER** .... [↵]
7. Press **ESC** .... [Esc]
   to remove graph and redisplay worksheet.

-Zooming a Graphic

NOTE: For temporarily viewing a graph.

1. Press : (Colon) .... [:]
   if you are not in the WYSIWYG menu.
2. Press **G** (Graph) .... [G]
3. Press **Z** (Zoom) .... [Z]

(continued)

4. Press **F3** (Name) F3
5. Highlight graph to be zoomed.
6. **ENTER** .... ↵
7. Press **ESC** .... Esc
   to remove graph and redisplay worksheet.

Previewing/Formatting/Printing a WYSIWYG Worksheet

NOTE: WYSIWYG does not support embedded setup strings entered through 1-2-3 commands. Remove all setup strings entered previously. To reset print settings to the default, press /P,P,C. It is recommended that the worksheet created with WYSIWYG be previewed before printing.

-Previewing

NOTE: If already working in the :Print submenu, steps 1-2 need not be repeated.

1. Press : (Colon) .... :
   if you are not in the WYSIWYG menu.
2. Press **P** (Print) .... P
3. Press **R** (Range) .... R
4. Press **S** (Set) .... S

(continued)

USING WYSIWYG (continued)

5. Type range to be printed.

6. **ENTER** .... ↵

7. Press **P** (Preview) .... P

8. Press **Spacebar**
   to exit preview mode. .... Space

-Formatting-Settings

NOTE: • If already working in the :Print submenu, steps 1-2 need not be repeated.
• This feature allows for changes in begin and end page numbers, copies to print, and whether to include grid or frame when printing.

1. Press : (Colon) .... :
   if you are not in the WYSIWYG menu.

2. Press **P** (Print) .... P

3. Press **S** (Settings) .... S

4. Select a setting option:

   -**B**egin .... B

   - Type first page number.
   - **ENTER** .... ↵

(continued)

-End .... E

- Type last page number.
- **ENTER** .... ↵

-Start-Number .... S

- Type page number for first page in print range.
- **ENTER** .... ↵

-Copies C

- Type number of copies to print.
- **ENTER** .... ↵

-Wait Waits at end of each page for paper change. .... W

- Type **No** or **Yes** .... N or Y

-Grid Prints grid lines in print range. .... G

- Type **No** or **Yes** .... N or Y

-Frame Prints frame with print range. .... F

- Type **No** or **Yes** .... N or Y

-Reset Returns print settings to default. .... R

-Quit Returns to previous menu. .... Q

(continued)

-Formatting-Layout

NOTE: If already working in the :Print submenu, steps 1-2 need not be repeated. This feature allows for changes in page size, margins, titles, borders, compression.

1. Press : (Colon) .... [:]
   if you are not in the WYSIWYG menu.
2. Press **P** (Print) .... [P]
3. Press **L** (Layout) .... [L]
4. Select a layout option:

   -**P**age-Size .... [P]

   - Select a page size:

     1-Letter (8 1/2"x11") .... [1]

     2-A4 .... [2]

     3-80"x66" .... [3]

     4-14"x11" .... [4]

     5-8 1/2"x12" .... [5]

     6-8 1/2" x 14 .... [6]

     7-6.9"x9.8" .... [7]

     C-Custom .... [C]

   - **ENTER** .... [↵]

(continued)

USING WYSIWYG (continued)

-Margins .... M

- Select margin to be affected:

  Left.. L

  Right....................................... R

  Top... T

  Bottom...................................... B

- Type new margin.
- **ENTER**....................................... ↵

-Titles .... T

- Highlight title to be affected:

  Header...................................... H

  Footer...................................... F

- Type header/footer text.
- **ENTER**....................................... ↵

-Border... B

- Select border to be affected:

  Top... T

  Left.. L

(continued)

USING WYSIWYG (continued)

- Type columns to print on top or left of each page.
- **ENTER**.. ↵

-**C**ompression.. C

- Select compression type:

None Removes manual or automatic compression... N

Manual Expands or compresses print range... M

- Type print compression ratio......................**Option**
- **ENTER**.. ↵

Automatic Compresses print range to fit on one page............ A

-Saving/Retrieving a Layout

NOTE: If already working in the :Print submenu, steps 1-2 need not be repeated.

1. Press : (Colon) .... :
   if you are not in the WYSIWYG menu.
2. Press **P** (Print).. P
3. Press **L** (Layout).. L

(continued)

4. Press **L** (Library) L
5. Press **S** (Save).. S

   -OR- OR

   Press **R** (Retrieve) .... R

   -OR- OR

   Press **E** (Erase).. E
6. Type name of layout file to be saved/retrieved.
7. **ENTER** .... ↵
   - If updating an existing library file:
   - Press **C** (Cancel)... C

   -OR- OR

   - Press **R** (Replace) .... R

-Printing

NOTE: If already working in the :Print submenu, steps 1-2 need not be repeated.

1. Press : (Colon) .... :
   if you are not in the WYSIWYG menu.

(continued)

2. Press **P** (Print).. P
3. Press **R** (Range).. R
4. Press **S** (Set).. S
5. Type range to be printed.
6. **ENTER**.. ↵
7. Press **G** (Go).. G
   to print current print range.

-Canceling/Changing a Print Range

1. Follow steps 1-2 above.
2. Press **R** (Range).. R
3. Press **S** (Set).. S
   - Type new print range.
   - **ENTER**.. ↵

     -OR- OR

   Press **C** (Clear).. C

(continued)

Entering and Editing Text in a WYSIWYG Worksheet

-Entering Text

NOTE: If already working in the :Print submenu, steps 1-2 need not be repeated.

1. Press : (Colon) .... :
   if you are not in the WYSIWYG menu.
2. Press **T** (Text) .... T
3. Press **E** (Edit).. E
4. Type range to receive text.
5. **ENTER** .... ↵

   Option: To enter text using a different font, press F3 and select desired font.
6. Type text into range.
7. Press **ESC** .... Esc

-Aligning Text

1. Follow steps 1-2 above.
3. Press **A** (Align) .... A

(continued)

USING WYSIWYG (continued)

4. Select an align option:

   Left L

   Right .... R

   Center C

   Even .... E

5. Type range to be aligned.

6. **ENTER** .... ↵

-Reformatting Text

NOTE: • *If already working in the :Print submenu, steps 1-2 need not be repeated.*
• *This feature will format long labels as a text range.*

1. Press : (Colon) .... :
   if you are not in the WYSIWYG menu.

2. Press **T** (Text) .... T

3. Press **R** (Reformat) .... R

4. Type range to be reformatted.

5. **ENTER** .... ↵

Changing Column Width and Row Height/Inserting Page Breaks in WYSIWYG Worksheet

NOTE: Lotus 1-2-3 measures row height in points. The row height default is 14 points. Lotus 1-2-3 will automatically adjust the height of a row to accommodate the largest font size in the row.

-Changing Column Width and Row Height

1. Press **:** (Colon) .... [:]
   if you are not in the WYSIWYG menu.
2. Press **W** (Worksheet) .... [W]
3. Press **C** (Column) .... [C]

   -S (Set-Width) .... [S]

   - Type columns to set width.
   - **ENTER** .... [↵]
   - Type number of characters for desired column width.
   - **ENTER** .... [↵]

   -R (Reset-Width) .... [R]

   - Type columns to reset width.
   - **ENTER** .... [↵]

   -OR-

(continued)

USING WYSIWYG (continued)

Press **R** (Row) .... R

-S (Set-Height) .... S

- Type rows to set height.
- **ENTER** .... ↵
- Type point size for desired row height.
- **ENTER** .... ↵

-Inserting/Deleting Page Breaks

1. Follow steps 1-2 on previous page.
2. Press **P** (Page) .... P
3. Place cursor at horizontal or vertical location to break page.
4. Select a page-break option:

Row	Inserts page break at row. ...	R
Column	Inserts page break at a column	C
Delete	Removes a page break	D
Quit	Returns to Ready Mode	Q

FUNCTION DESCRIPTIONS

@@

Returns contents of cell or range address.

@ABS

Calculates the absolute (positive value) of X.

@ACOS

Calculates the arc cosine of a value.

@ASIN

Calculates the arc sine of a value.

@ATAN

Calculates the arc tangent of a value.

@ATANS

Calculates the four-quadrant arc tangent of y/x.

@AVG

Averages values in a list.

@CELL

Produces information about an **attribute** for the first cell in a range.

@CELL POINTER

Produces information about an **attribute** for the current cell.

(continued)

FUNCTION DESCRIPTIONS (continued)

@CHAR

Indicates the Lotus International Character Set equivalent which code X produces.

@CHOOSE

Finds the value or string in a list that is specified by the offset number.

@CLEAN

Eliminates non-printable characters such as ASCII codes from character string.

@CODE

Indicates the Lotus International Character Set code which corresponds to the first character in a string.

@COLS

Counts the number of columns in a range.

@COORD

Creates absolute, mixed, or relative reference from provided values.

@COS

Calculates the cosine of x angle which is measured in radians. The answer results in a value from -1 to 1.

(continued)

FUNCTION DESCRIPTIONS (continued)

@COUNT

Counts and indicates the nonblank cells in a list. Cells containing values as well as labels are counted.

@CTERM

Computes the number of periods required for an investment (present value) to increase to a **future value,** earning a fixed **interest** rate per period.

@DATE

Calculates the date number for the specified year, month and day.

@DATEVALUE

Calculates the date number for a string entered as a date.

@DAVG

A database function that averages values in a field of the input range that meets criteria range.

@DAY

Calculates the day of the month in the date number.

@DCOUNT

A database function that counts and indicates nonblank cells in a field of the input range that meet criteria in the criteria range.

(continued)

FUNCTION DESCRIPTIONS (continued)

@DDB

Using the double-declining balance method, calculates the depreciation allowance of an asset for a specified period.

@DGET

A database function that uses criteria to find value or label in database table.

@DMAX

A database function that finds and indicates the largest value in a field of the input range that meets the criteria in the criteria range.

@DMIN

A database function that finds and indicates the smallest value in a field of the input range that meets the criteria in the criteria range.

@DQUERY

A database function that sends external database command.

@DSTD

A database function that calculates the standard deviation of the values in a field of an input range that meets the criteria in the criteria range.

(continued)

FUNCTION DESCRIPTIONS (continued)

@DSTDS

A database function that calculates the sample standard deviation of the values in the field of an input range that meets the criteria in the criteria range.

@DSUM

A database functions that sums the values in a field of an input range that meet the criteria in the criteria range.

@D360

A database function that calculates days between two date numbers.

@DVAR

A database function that calculates the variance of values in a field of an input range that meet the criteria in the criteria range.

@DVARS

A database function that calculates the sample variance in the field of an input range that meet the criteria in the criteria range.

@ERR

Indicates an error message (ERR) if a wrong value is entered. The function is usually used with @IF to indicate an error value.

(continued)

FUNCTION DESCRIPTIONS (continued)

@EXACT

Compares string1 with string2 and indicates 1 if true (they are the same), 0 if false (they are not the same).

@EXP

Calculates the value of e raised to the power x.

@FALSE

Produces a 0 (false) as a logical value.

@FIND

Calculates the position in a string in which the first occurrence of a search-string is found.

@FV

Calculates the future value of an investment at the end of each period which is compounded at the periodic interest rate.

@HLOOKUP

Find the contents of a cell in the highlighted row of a horizontal lookup table.

@HOUR

Calculated the hour in integer form.

(continued)

FUNCTION DESCRIPTIONS (continued)

@IF

Answers a true/false question and calculated data according to the answer.

@INDEX

Locates the value from within a range.

@INFO

Reports System information.

@INT

Produces the integer part of a value.

@IRR

Calculates the rate of return expected from a series of cash flows generated by an investment.

@ISERR

Tests x for the an error value and returns 1 if true, 0 if false.

@ISNA

Tests x for NA value and returns 1 if true, 0 if false.

@ISNUMBER

Tests x for a value and returns 1 (true) if x is a value or a blank cell and returns 0 (false) if x is a string.

(continued)

FUNCTION DESCRIPTIONS (continued)

@ISRANGE

Determines whether argument is valid range name or range address.

@ISSTRING

Tests x for a string and returns 1 (true) if x is a literal string containing a label or sting formula and returns 0 (false) if x is a value or blank cell.

@LEFT

Indicates the first n character in string.

@LENGTH

Counts the number of characters in a string.

@LN

Calculates the natural logarithm of x.

@LOG

Calculates the common logarithm (base 10) of x.

@LOWER

Converts uppercase letters in a string to lowercase letters.

@MAX

Finds and indicates the largest value in a list.

(continued)

FUNCTION DESCRIPTIONS (continued)

@MID

Indicates in characters from string beginning with the character at start-number. The first start number in a string is 0.

@MIN

Finds and indicated the lowest value in a list.

@MINUTE

Calculates minutes in integer form in time-number.

@MOND

Calculates the remainder of x/y.

@MONTH

Extracts the month in integer form from the date-number.

@N

Indicates the entry in the first cell in a range as a value and returns the value if the cell contains a value and returns a 0 if the cell does not contain a value.

@NA

Produces an NA (not available) value.

@NOW

Produces the current date and time.

(continued)

FUNCTION DESCRIPTIONS (continued)

@NPV

Calculates the net present value of a series of future cash flows discounted at a fixed, interest rate.

@PI

Returns the value π. π is the ratio of the circumference of a circle to its diameter.

@PMT

Calculates the amount of the periodic payment needed to pay off a loan using a specified periodic interest rate and number of payment periods.

@PROPER

Converts the letter in a string to initial caps for the first letter of each word an lower case for remaining letters.

@PV

Calculates the present value of an investment based on a series of payments discounted at a periodic interest rate over he number of periods in term.

@RAND

Indicates a random value between 0 and 1.

@RATE

Calculates periodic interest rate necessary for payments (present value) to grow to a future value specified term.

(continued)

FUNCTION DESCRIPTIONS (continued)

@REPEAT

Repeats characters in a cell which is not limited to the cell width. The label prefix \ (backslash) followed by a character will repeat labels to fill one cell. @REPEAT is not limited to the column width.

@REPLACE

Replaces n characters in the original string with the new string beginning at the start number.

@RIGHT

Indicates the last n characters in a string.

@ROUND

Rounds a value to a specified number of places.

@ROWS

Counts the number of rows in a range.

@S

Indicates the entry in the first cell in a range as a label and returns the label if the cell contains a label and returns 0 if the cell does not contain a label.

@SECOND

Calculates the seconds in integer form in time-number.

(continued)

FUNCTION DESCRIPTIONS (continued)

@SHEETS

Counts the worksheets in a range.

@SIN

Calculates the sine of a x angle measured in radians.

@SLN

Calculates the straight-line depreciation allowance of an asset for one period.

@SQRT

Calculates the positive square root of a value or 0.

@STD

Calculates the standard deviation of values in a list.

@STDS

Calculates the sample standard deviation of values in a list.

@STRING

Converts the x value into a string with specified decimal places.

@SUM

Adds values in a list.

(continued)

FUNCTION DESCRIPTIONS (continued)

@SUMPRODUCT

Adds the product of values in a list.

@SYD

Calculates the sum-of-the-years' digits depreciation allowance of an asset for a specified period.

@TAN

Calculates the tangent of x angle measured in radians.

@TERM

Calculates the number of payment period necessary to reach future value, when the investment earns a periodic interest rate.

@TIME

Calculates the time number for the specified hour, minutes and seconds.

@TIMEVALUE

Calculates the time number for a string that looks like a time.

@TRIM

Removes leading, trailing and consecutive spaces from a string.

(continued)

FUNCTION DESCRIPTIONS (continued)

@TRUE

Produces a 1 (true) as a logical value.

@UPPER
Converts lowercase letters in a string to uppercase letters.

@VALUE

Converts a number entered as a string to its corresponding value.

@VAR

Calculates variance of values in a list.

@VARS

Calculates sample variance of values in a list.

@VDB

Calculates depreciation using double-declining balance method, and allows the percentage of straight-line depreciation to be non-200% values.

@VLOOKUP

Finds the contents of a cell in the highlighted column of a horizontal lookup table.

@YEAR

Calculates the year in integer form in date-number.

MACRO COMMANDS and DESCRIPTIONS

NOTE: Macro Commands are listed alphabetically by key word. Descriptions follow each command.

{?}

Temporarily stops macro.

{ABS}

Changes a cell or range of cells from relative to absolute to mixed values.

{ADDIN}

Displays a menu of add-in programs.

{APP1,APP2,APP3,APP4}

Invokes add-in programs.

{APPENDBELOW} and **{APPENDRIGHT}**

Attaches data from a specified source below or to the right of a specified target.

{BACKSPACE} or **{BS}**

Instructs 1-2-3 to move back a space.

{BEEP}

Sounds a tone to get the user's attention.

(continued)

{BIGLEFT} and {BIGRIGHT}

Moves the cursor one page to the left or to the right.

{BLANK}

Erases cell content, but not the cell format.

{BRANCH}

Transfers control the current macro to another part of a macro. Commonly used in "If"/"Then" arguments.

{BREAK}

Returns computer to the ready mode. Equivalent to pressing ESCAPE.

{BREAKOFF} and {BREAKON}

Disables/Enables CTRL-BREAK.

{CALC}

In ready mode, recalculates formulas in a worksheet; in VALUE and EDIT modes, converts a formula to its current value.

{CE}

Clears prompt information.

{CLOSE}

Closes a previously opened text file.

(continued)

MACROS (continued)

{CONTENTS}

Copies value contents of a source-location cell to a target-location as a label.

{DEFINE}

Operates as a subroutine in retrieving data and returning it as a result.

{DELETE} and **{DEL}**

Instructs 1-2-3 to press the DEL button.

{DOWN} and **{D}**

Instructs 1-2-3 to access the "down arrow" action.

{EDIT}

Instructs 1-2-3 to access the F2 (EDIT) action.

{END}

Instructs 1-2-3 to access the END action.

{ESCAPE} and **{ESC}**

Instructs 1-2-3 to access the ESC action.

{FILE}

Turns on file status indicator.

{FILESIZE}

Counts the file size before reading it. Use OPEN text file before using FILESIZE.

(continued)

MACROS (continued)

{FIRSTCELL} and **{FC}**

Moves cell pointer to A:A1 in active file.

{FIRSTFILE} and **{FF}**

Moves cell pointer to last highlighted cell in first active file.

{FOR}

Starts a "for-next" loop a repeated number of times.

{FORBREAK}

Cancels a "for-next" loop.

{FORM}

Temporarily stops the macro so data can be entered or edited.

{FORMBREAK}

Ends a FORM command.

{FRAMEOFF} and **{FRAMEON}**

Same as BORDERSOFF and BORDERSON.

{GET}

Interrupts a macro until a key is pressed. The key is then recorded in the specified location.

{GETLABEL}

Interrupts a macro, prompts the user to type information as a label and stores it.

(continued)

MACROS (continued)

{GETNUMBER}

Interrupts a macro, prompts the user to type information as a value and stores it.

{GOTO}

Instructs 1-2-3 to go to a specific cell or range.

{GRAPH}

Displays a graph while the macro pauses.

{GRAPHON} and {GRAPHOFF}

Displays the graph and removes the graph while the macro is running.

{HELP}

Temporarily stops the macro so user can access Help.

{HOME}

Places the cursor at the home position.

{IF}

Creates a conditional statement.

{INDICATE}

Replaces READY mode with "string."

{INSERT} and {INS}

Instructs 1-2-3 to insert a space.

(continued)

MACROS (continued)

{LASTCELL} and **{LC}**

Moves cell pointer to end of active area in current file.

{LASTFILE} and **{LF}**

Moves cell pointer to last highlighted cell in last active file.

{LEFT} and **{L}**

Instructs 1-2-3 to move the cursor left.

{LET}

Inserts a label or value in a specified location.

{LOOK}

Instructs 1-2-3 to look for a particular response by the user before continuing with the macro. Used before BRANCH.

{MENU}

Instructs 1-2-3 to display the menu.

{MENUBRANCH}

Displays the menu and waits for user's selection. Each selection is a branch in the macro. After the macro completes the instructions associated with user's selection, the macro ends.

{MENUCALL}

Same as MENUBRANCH. However, after the macro completes the instructions associated with user's selection, the macro continues from the command following MENUCALL.

(continued)

MACROS (continued)

{NAME}

Lists named ranges in the POINT mode.

{NEXTFILE} and {NF}

Moves cell pointer to last highlighted cell in next active file.

{NEXTSHEET} and {NS}

Moves cell pointer to next worksheet.

{ONERROR}

Displays an error message if an error occurs while the macro is running.

{OPEN}

Opens a file on disk and allows the user access to read, write, modify or append the file.

{PANELOFF} and {PANELON}

Turns off panel so user cannot see the series of steps made by the macro to complete its task.

{PGDN} and {PGUP}

Instructs 1-2-3 to move down and up one page.

{PREVFILE} and {PF}

Moves cell pointer to last highlighted cell in previous active file.

(continued)

MACROS (continued)

{PREVSHEET} and **{PS}**

Moves cell pointer to previous worksheet.

{PUT}

Places selected data in a cell in a desired range.

{QUERY}

Repeats last DATA/QUERY specified when 1-2-3 is in READY mode.

{QUIT}

Terminates the macro.

{READ}

Copies specified number of characters from text file to a specified location.

{READLN}

Copies a particular line from text file and stores its characters in a specified location.

{RECALC} and **{RECALCCOL}**

Recalculates values in a desired range, row by row or column by column.

{RESTART}

Cancels a subroutine and instructs 1-2-3 to continue to the next command in the macro.

(continued)

MACROS (continued)

{RETURN}

Returns macro control from a subroutine to the current macro.

{RIGHT} and {R}

Instructs 1-2-3 to move cursor right.

{SETPOS}

Sets the byte pointer position of the offset-number in an open text file.

{SUBROUTINE}

Divides the macro into smaller separate tasks.

{SYSTEM}

Pauses the macro while it handles a specified task in DOS.

{TABLE}

Repeats last DATA/TABLE specified when 1-2-3 is in READY mode.

{UP} and {U}

Instructs 1-2-3 to move cursor up.

{WAIT}

Pauses the macro for a specified time. During the pause, the WAIT indicator light will be displayed.

(continued)

MACROS (continued)

{WINDOWSOFF}

Disables screen display.

{WINDOWSON}

Turns on screen display.

{WRITE}

Copies a string to the current cell in text file.

{WRITELN}

Writes a string at the current cell in text file which includes a carriage return and line feed.

{ZOOM}

Toggles worksheet between full-screen and original size.

FUNCTION KEYS

KEY	KEY NAME	FUNCTION PERFORMER
F1	HELP	Accesses Help menu.
F2	EDIT	In READY mode, puts Lotus 1-2-3 in EDIT mode to enable cell contents to be edited.
F3	NAME	In POINT mode, displays a list of named ranges. Lists @functions or advanced macro commands for formulas and macros.
F4	ABS(olute)	Changes a cell or range of cells from relative to absolute to mixed values.
F5	GOTO	In READY mode, moves cursor directly to new cell location specified.
F6	WINDOW	Moves cursor between windows during screen split.
F7	QUERY	In READY mode, repeats last DATA/QUERY specified.
F8	TABLE	In READY mode, repeats last DATA/TABLE specified.
F9	CALC	In READY mode, recalculates formulas in a worksheet; In VALUE and EDIT modes, converts a formula to its current value.
F10	GRAPH	Displays graph with current settings.

(continued)

FUNCTION KEYS (continued)

Keys	Name	Description
Alt + F1	COMPOSE	In READY, EDIT and LABEL modes, creates international characters that cannot be entered directly from keyboard.
Alt + F2	RECORD	Records macro and turns STEP mode on to execute macros one step at a time.
Alt + F3	RUN	In READY mode, displays list of macro names for selecting a macro to run.
Alt + F4	UNDO	In READY mode, cancels any changes made to worksheet. Pressing Alt+F4 again will restore changes.
Alt + F6	ZOOM	Toggles worksheets between their full-size and original size.
Alt + F7	APP1	In READY mode, accesses add-in program assigned to key.
Alt + F8	APP2	In READY mode, accesses add-in program assigned to key.
Alt + F9	APP3	In READY mode, accesses add-in program assigned to key.
Alt + F10	APP4	In READY mode, displays add-in menu and accesses add-in program assigned to key.

GLOSSARY

Absolute Value

A term used in the copying process to indicate reproduction of a cell without change. Sometimes referred to as "no change."

Add-Ins

Special Programs that can be used with LOTUS 1-2-3 to extend its capabilities.

Cell

A single location on a worksheet.

Cell Address

A column letter and row number, e.g., A1 or F12.

Column

The vertical portions of the worksheet, e.g. A, B, C, etc. There are 256 columns in a worksheet.

Column Width

A term used to refer to the size of a cell. A cell may be made wider or narrower from the default size of 9 characters.

Cursor

The cell pointer.

Copying

Reproducing data from one location to another.

Data Range

The range of values used to create a graph.

Default

The present conditions of LOTUS 1-2-3 which may be modified. For example: column width settings.

(continued)

GLOSSARY (continued)

Editing
Changing the contents of a cell.

Field Names
Column headings (labels) that appear in the first row of a database which identify the content of each column.

File
A collection of saved worksheets.

File Name
The name given to a collection of shared worksheet(s).

Font
Characters available in a typeface in varying sizes and/or styles which may be used in WYSIWYG to change the appearance of the printed worksheet or graph.

Formatting
Using special function commands to display worksheet data.

Function
A built-in formula that performs calculations or special operations.

Global
A command affecting the entire worksheet.

Graphing
Preparing a visual interpretation of data in the form of bar, XY, high-low-close-open, line, mixed, stacked bar graph or pie chart.

(continued)

GLOSSARY (continued)

Label
The column and row headings or titles that begin with a letter or label prefix.

Label Prefix
Characters that precede the label to control label alignment.

Link
A formula refers to data in another (spreadsheet) file.

Local
A command that changes a specific portion of the worksheet.

Logical Function
An @function that answers a true/false question and calculates data according to the answer.

Logical Operator
Symbols such as > <, #AND#, and #OR# used in logical formulas to evaluate equality and inequality.

Macro
A series of recorded keystrokes that automates a LOTUS task.

Map
Shows location of formulas, values, annotated numbers, numbers, and labels designated by #, +, and " symbols.

Perspective
Shows "3D" screen of three consecutive worksheets.

(continued)

GLOSSARY (continued)

Range
A cell or a rectangular group of adjacent cells in the worksheet, or a collection of ranges in contiguous worksheets in the same file.

Range Address
The location of a range in a worksheet: A3..D5.

Range Name
A name given to identify a range on a worksheet or in contiguous worksheets in the same file.

Record
A LOTUS 1-2-3 feature used to create macros.

Relative
A term used in the copy process to indicate the automatic change of the cell references in the formula to adapt to the new location.

Retrieve
The process of accessing a saved file.

Row
The horizontal portion of a worksheet. e.g. 1,2,3, etc. There are 8,192 rows in a worksheet.

Save
Stores a copy of the worksheet on disk.

Setup String
Characters preceded by a \ that directs the printer to print in a certain way.

(continued)

GLOSSARY (continued)

Scroll

A vertical or horizontal cursor movement which will display portions of the spreadsheet that exist beyond the limits of the screen.

Sort

The process of arranging records in a database in a particular order according to the contents of one field.

Value

A numerical or formula entry on the worksheet used in calculations.

Window

A software command to split the spreadsheet horizontally or vertically into separate scrollable worksheets.

Worksheet

A columnar spreadsheet containing 256 columns and 8,192 rows used to calculate or analyze data.

COMMAND INDEX

Copy Command

Data Commands

File Commands

Graph Commands

(continued)

COMMAND INDEX (continued)

Move Command

Print Commands

Quit Command

Range Commands

(continued)

COMMAND INDEX (continued)

System Command

Worksheet Command

WYSIWYG COMMANDS

Display Commands

Format Commands

Graph Commands

Print Commands

(continued)

WYSIWYG COMMANDS (continued)

Text Commands

Worksheet Commands

INDEX

(continued)

INDEX (continued)

(continued)

INDEX (continued)

(continued)

INDEX (continued)

(continued)

INDEX (continued)

(continued)

INDEX (continued)

(continued)

INDEX (continued)

P

Q

R

S

(continued)

INDEX (continued)

(continued)

INDEX (continued)

W

(continued)

INDEX (continued)

(continued)